HANGING BY A THREAD

Mark Rutland

CREATION
HOUSE
LAKE MARY, FLORIDA

Creation House
Strang Communications Company
600 Rinehart Road
Lake Mary, FL 32746
(407) 333-0600

First printing, November 1991
Second printing, March 1992

This book is dedicated to my mother,
Rosemary Hance Rutland.

"Who can find a virtuous woman?
for her price is far above rubies."
Proverbs 31:10

ACKNOWLEDGMENTS

I want to thank those whose personal contributions have helped in the preparation of this book. I am indebted to Gordon Miller, Julie Culwell, Walter Walker and my mother, Rosemary Rutland, for their help in manuscript preparation and editing. They all deserve special recognition.

I thank my wife and children for their patience, understanding and encouragement, and I thank the members of Calvary Assembly in Winter Park, Florida, for praying diligently for their pastor.

CONTENTS

FOREWORD

A number of great revivals have swept across our nation. The effects of some have even reached all the way around the world. In each one of these spiritual awakenings, the Holy Spirit has halted a downward spiral of corruption. He revived the spiritual life in the church and restrained the erosion of virtue in society.

Unbelief, immorality and a general disregard for Christian values are not unique to our day. The world and the church have been in very bad situations before. Some say it's worse than ever. Maybe that's so. But whether or not our society is more depraved than in other generations, this truth remains: As Christian virtues are forgotten or distorted, society deteriorates, and community eventually turns into chaos.

Today we live in one of those times in history where the whole concept of virtue is becoming so warped that it is no longer a matter of men and women choosing wrong over right — they don't know which is which any more. Politicians, educators, business leaders — the movers of society — morally cannot tell their right hands from their left hands.

The world has taken the concept of courage and misconstrued it to be cruelty. It has taken diligence and distorted it into obsessiveness. It has taken meekness and turned it into "wimpiness." Qualities that for generations have been esteemed as noble are now mocked. A man who sacrifices all for a principle is a sucker. A young person who remains morally pure is ridiculed.

The standards for value and virtue are rapidly changing. Our whole culture is like a ship lost at sea. The crew that is being carried along with it knows they are a long way from where they are supposed to be. They have no idea where their present course will lead them. Neither do they have the slightest notion of how to get back to where they came from.

It is scary to be lost at sea not knowing where you are or where you are going. Sometimes when you do know where you are headed, it is even more frightening. Without the revival of Christian virtue, the prevailing social order will disintegrate, removing the one thing that keeps us from living like barbarians.

Alexis de Tocqueville came to America in the early days of the republic. He observed: America is great because America is good. If it ceases to be good, it will cease to be great. It is less likely that we will be bombed into the Stone Age than it is that we will arrive there because of the loss of Christian values. More precisely, it is the depraved distortion and redefining of what is virtuous that manifests itself as the clear and present danger.

Jesus said to His followers that they were the salt of the earth. Christians are to be that element in society that preserves truth, human dignity and goodness. When, however, the church has preached virtue, it has too often focused on rules instead of reasons. Modesty isn't about clothing; it's about attracting people to God instead of to us. Frugality isn't about dressing in rags and pinching pennies; it's about placing the proper value on things we need and use.

Law without life has little appeal to average men and women today. They have no more taste for it than they do for salt without savor. Christians need to come out from under the bushel of conformity which covers too many believers and hides the light of God's glory. It is time for integrity that springs, not merely from rule-keeping, but from a true, intimate relationship with the living God.

Salt is not what you do — it's what you are. A virtuous man preserves that which is good in society, often without consciously trying to do so. Just his presence there reveals the darkness in men's hearts and exposes their perverted attempts to make evil look like good. He is an example that reminds people what goodness is all about, regardless of whether they choose to follow.

What would it be like for a generation that had no such example? What kind of twisted view of morality would they have, and what kind of society would be the result?

It's time for one of those spiritual and moral awakenings. Francis Frangipane recently said: "The 1980s may have been the time for *incredible* ministries. This is the time for *credible* ministries."

Mark Rutland has taken a long, hard look at Christian

virtues — something we all need to do. He is one of today's most gifted communicators, and his message is truly a word from God for all believers in times like these. Grasp the truths contained in this book; live them out; and pass them on.

Christians cannot govern their lives with the world's "new sense" of virtue. Too much is at stake. We *are* the salt of the earth. We *are* the light of the world.

James Robison
Fort Worth, Texas

I

THE THREAD OF VIRTUE

Through the tinted windows of the fifteenth floor, he stared down at the miniature parking lot far beneath him. Tiny men the size of insects climbed in and out of toy BMWs. He knew none of them could see him. He was absolutely secure behind the sterile, opaque glass shields. He indulged himself in one brief run-through of that familiar, comforting mental checklist of his attire. Perfect! He was sure of that in a split second. Delicately knotted paisley tie, tailored silk shirt hugging his health-club-tightened torso, British woolen trousers celebrating a gentle break halfway between his knees and his Italian shoes. A faint flicker of a smile danced across his tanned face. Reassured, he turned to face the men waiting behind him.

He moved his gaze from face to face before he announced his decision: "We'll just lie to them." He enunciated each syllable calmly as if by saying it slowly he could affirm his own lack of shame. "Tell them we had a momentary technical breakdown at our New England factory. That will give us time to get our brief filed in Los Angeles court. By the time they wake up, there will be nothing they can do."

The future of the West hangs by a thread. ...The thread is virtue.

A reverent murmur of admiration seemed to roll up involuntarily from those men watching him, waiting to see him spring into action. He knew he had not failed them. They had seen the lethal, bolt-action use of power for which he was becoming famous. This was what they came for. They had seen. They had learned. As they turned to leave, their genuine-leather soles scuffling against the Persian carpet sounded rather like the padded paws of wolves on crisp snow. ■

The future of the West hangs by a thread. That single strand is tied to the edge of a platform jutting out over the abyss of evil. Dangling haplessly above the chasm of human nightmare is the wounded remnant of a once-noble culture.

The thread is virtue. Misunderstood or neglected virtue rots. The gravitational power of brutality threatens to break the thread and plunge goodness into the darkness of a frozen hell. The platform of hope above it, like the immovable, golden floor of heaven, is just visible. Society can painstakingly ascend the rope of virtue to a place where it can at least see light. Or it can loose its hold and sink into the pit called despair.

The point is that there is no other way up and no hope at all below. If a society chooses its virtues wrongly, the beast below gains strength. The constant cosmic downward pressure becomes a shocking jerk on the frail string, threatening to pop it loose altogether. The horror of a culture that has broken the thread of virtue and dropped into the yawning mouth of societal nightmare is not an unprecedented historical theory.

In the tattered rags of history's broken societies are found the golden threads of distant and long-forgotten virtues. These virtues were bastardized and perverted beyond recognition as the downward pull became too strong for the thread.

When virtue unravels, the joyless, bitter winter of soullessness brings cruel famine upon the land. That is when they come creeping out of the trees. They are men like wolves in the snow. Harsh, merciless and beastly, they are ravenous and rapacious. They devour. They destroy. Constantly on the attack, they even watch for their own to stumble or show a sign of weakness.

These monstrous beasts of prey now freely prowl the West's frozen landscape. Virtueless, they are the fruit of us. Merciless, they are the death of us.

A number of years ago Dr. Karl Menninger wrote *Whatever Became of Sin?*[1] The book was a call to personal accountability. To be sure, Menninger did not believe that sin itself had disappeared. He referred to the virtual disappearance of the concept and the word from our vocabulary. He meant, "Whatever became of the idea of sin?" — not that we are short of it.

With this book I am asking another question: Whatever

became of virtue? I do not mean merely the idea of virtue. But where is the actual virtue? Is there buried under the snow the half-frozen bulb of dormant virtue? The whole concept of virtuous living has become so alien to Western culture that until — and unless — we recapture it, our society may well be doomed.

All too often now our society has tended to think of virtue as a quality desirable only for women. We are led to think that women should be virginal and good — at least the ones men marry. But men are to be somehow above such sissy notions. Such thinking may be convenient for men, but it betrays a tragic lack of understanding of true virtue.

The very word "virtue" derives from the Latin word for strength. The connotation is of straining, as the muscles of a man might strain at the confines of a too-tight shirt. In other words, virtue is restrained strength. It actually implies manliness. It is that strength, that power, by which one physical body affects another. In medicine there is a classical use of the word virtue. The virtue of a plant, for example, is that power inherent in it to produce medicine. Virtue also relates to the medicine itself. There is virtue in the medicine for healing. Mixture, adulteration, dilution or exposure may diminish the virtue.

In the eighth chapter of his Gospel, Luke used virtue to connote power. A woman with an abnormal flow of blood came near to Jesus, struggling in the crowd just to touch His garment. Jesus announced to those around Him that someone had touched Him. In wild, unruly jostling, such a statement seemed absurd. How could He tell one touch from another? Jesus explained that He felt *virtue* flow out of Him.

There is power in virtue and virtue in power. Resident in a virtuous man is inestimable power to impact for good those around him. Just as there is healing power in virtuous living, virtueless living is a fountain of poison. The virtueless man is a spring of death because many people — wife, children, employees — drink at every man's fountain.

The Downward Spiral

Every society anchors its ideals in its virtues. If those virtues are good, it is ennobled. It grows into the image of its linchpin virtues. When those virtues are absent or perverted, there will be a downward spiral in the values, actions and character of its people.

The very word "virtue" derives from the Latin word for strength.

The real danger is not the absence of virtue. There is no historical evidence of an utterly virtueless society. The great danger is not the lack of any virtue. It is wrong virtues! It is tragic when men who understand virtue act in virtueless ways. But the real danger is redefining virtue as evil and evil as virtue. When that happens, the very thread which holds civilization intact is threatened.

In ancient Rome the preeminent virtue was bravery. But Roman bravery, misunderstood and untempered by Christian love, soon became brutal and callous. Similarly, in communist Russia, for many years, the zenith of all virtue was loyalty to the state. That virtue was perverted into a lethal poison that pumped shattered lives into Siberia like the toxic waste of systemic atheism. The state expected its citizens to betray family members even if it meant death or imprisonment. Stalin professed that any lie, any act of treachery, any form of violence was acceptable — even virtuous — in the cause of communism. Torture, deceit and murder were not seen as violations of virtue. Instead they actually became the vehicles by which Stalin's preeminent virtue was celebrated.

As a society defines its virtues, it in turn is defined by those virtues. Twisted virtue means twisted culture. Suppose, for example, a certain society hates failure, ugliness, obesity and stupidity. The premier virtues might then be success, slim beauty and intelligence. If, therefore, beauty itself is a virtue, then all is permissible if I can achieve beauty, associate with beauty or cause beauty to be.

The downward spiral might go something like this:

1) Beauty as an abstract ascends as a societal virtue.

2) If beauty is a virtue, ugliness is despisable.

3) If ugliness is despisable, ugly people are worth less than beautiful people.

4) If beautiful people are worth more than ugly people, it is not as bad to murder the ugly.

5) Therefore murdering ugly people is a virtue.

Furthermore, by such a perverted spiral a society might embrace even murder in the pursuit of beauty. Some may object that such a scenario is bizarre and farfetched. It is, in fact, quite reasonable.

The society in which beauty is the highest and best virtue could easily degenerate to the point where pornography would be held in higher regard than the Bible. Or, for example, imagine a society so degraded that art of any kind would be held in higher regard than chastity or mercy. That society might well permit or even commission its artists to produce the most heinous kind of evil in the name of art. A state that will subsidize urine portraits of Jesus might allow portraits of Mary painted in the blood of virgins. Murder for art may not be as farfetched as we think.

Imagine a society in which selfishness is a virtue. Ayn Rand's *The Virtue of Selfishness* envisioned and fostered such a culture in the West.[2] She was a prophetess of the wolves among us today. The exaltation of selfishness to the status of a virtue threatens the thread and initiates the downward spiral something like this:

1) Doing it my way (selfishness) is a virtue.

2) If selfishness is a virtue, doing "it" just to benefit others is a vice.

3) Therefore whatever inconveniences me is wrong.

4) Therefore to murder an inconvenient unborn child is a justifiable and even virtuous deed.

Marguerite Hardy thought she herself was the best nurse she knew. She glanced at a pretty, young nurse standing near the charts and sniffed her disapproval. Marguerite detested these new nurses and their casual, unstarched folksiness. They seemed to her like go-go dancers pretending to be nurses. What an irreverent travesty! To Marguerite there was nothing higher, holier perhaps, than the sterile execution of her duties.

Nurse Hardy was a vestal virgin of her own goddess. The soft, rhythmic squeak of nursing shoes on the tile floors of the clinic were sacramental. She dispensed pills and paper cups like bread and wine. Her uniform was a clerical robe. Her stethoscope was a stole.

"Ms. Hardy, bring in Jenny Jones," said Dr. Killdear, his voice shattering her reverie.

"Yes, doctor," she answered crisply and marched toward the waiting room.

Nurse Hardy entered the waiting room like Nero entering one of his prisons. She relished the surge of power she felt when these pitiful, wilted little rabbits quivered at her voice.

"Jenny Jones, you're next," she announced.

The wretched little thing literally shivered. How Marguerite Hardy resented these girls. They were pregnant simply because they lacked her stone resolve to live out a cold rebellion against disgusting male ardor. They probably deserved to have to give birth. It would serve them right.

But, then again, that was exactly the point of this clinic. It was a kind of chapel to Marguerite. To her, this was not just one abortion after another. It was worship. The goddess of self-determination must have blood. Her goddess demanded her daily diet of fleshy shreds sucked out of the bodies of these lesser beings. By helping, assisting in the rites, Marguerite celebrated her own liberty from the old male god of her grandmother. ■

Virtue and Vitality

If a society hopes to elevate or ennoble its character, it must carefully define its virtues. The most basic values held by a society dictate the kind of leaders it will produce. If the premier values are hard work, perseverance, creativity, ingenuity and discipline, it produces men like George Washington Carver. On the other hand, if the preeminent virtue is flamboyant wealth — no matter how you get it — it produces an Ivan Boesky. In our country, alas, we lean toward believing pretty strongly that the virtues of our grandparents produce hard-working suckers.

A recent survey of mothers of school-age children was conducted in both Japan and the United States. It asked this question: What do you consider the most important variable in a child's success in school? By far the largest number of American mothers thought it to be intelligence. Almost 100 percent of the Japanese mothers, however, answered work and diligence.

I remember a shocking experience of teaching heroism to a group of American school children. I began by explaining the plot of an old Western movie, *High Noon*. I told them the story of the hero who single-handedly, for the sake of a cowardly, undeserving town, faces a whole gang of outlaws. His bride, a nice enough girl, will not admire or stand by him and declares that she believes him to be a fool. Then I told them of the moment of truth when, all alone, our hero must settle things in the street.

"What do you think of a guy like that?" I asked.

One ten-year-old boy answered at once, "Whatta sucker!"

The most basic values held by a society dictate the kind of leaders it will produce.

I cringed. That child had already begun to redefine the virtue of courage so that, in his mind, it no longer included selfless love. I wondered if I could explain the courage of the cross to that boy.

The teenager who makes rebellion a virtue imitates rebellious men. The way he stands and dresses, what he does and refuses to do, the things he will and will not endure betray his real virtues.

The businessman who sells tainted baby food to a Third World country without a qualm knows that his society has defined a virtue called success without integrity. A congressman who makes power a virtue sells his soul for votes, awaiting the crest of every political poll like an ideological surfer. It is the fragile thread of virtue that separates men from the beasts.

Likewise, the prevailing winds of virtue greatly impact whether the church in a society produces an Elmer Gantry or a John Wesley. If that which we as a people admire is flamboyant success in a worldly sense, the local pastor must live on the highest level of personal commitment to virtue, or he will succumb to this lowest level of ambition.

There is always pressure to invite into his pulpit "Christian superstars" whose methods and theology are in direct contradiction to his own. He will feel the constant drag of materialism's anchor-rope every time he preaches holiness.

The teenager who stands by the side of the road with a sign reading "THERE IS NOTHING WORTH DYING FOR" is drowning in selfishness. Now there may well be nothing worth killing for. That is a different thing. But "There is nothing worth dying for" is the motto of beastly instinct. Survive at any cost! What does that say about Calvary? There must be things or ideas worth dying for. If not, the cross is a sick joke, and Tiananmen Square was a fools' parade.

All the great decisions of any society will be dictated by how it defines its virtues. A woman in New England recently shot to death her four-year-old-son. Though she was found guilty, her judge probated the five-year sentence. The judge said that while it was indeed murder, it was mitigated by the fact that the boy was retarded. Now is the winter of our discontent! America is staring into the abyss when such legal decisions concerning the fundamental sanctity of life are handed down by those whose senses of virtue and priority are based upon expediency and convenience.

Some years ago I engaged in a radio debate about abortion. My opponent was a pro-choice rabbi. He explained that he rejected the old idea of the value of life. He calmly announced that he now held "quality of life" to be a higher ideal. I was stunned! I could hardly look at him. It was hard to believe what I was hearing. I asked if he realized that he had just uttered the same words used by the Nazi judges to justify the forced sterilization of the retarded and the killing of the Jews and Gypsies. He was furious, of course, and the debate lost all hope of any usefulness.

Afterward, in the parking lot, the rabbi screamed at me, "Are you daring to call *me* a Nazi?" I assured him I was not, but I went on to say that the world is topside-down when rabbis think like Nazis.

Something was terribly wrong with his reasoning. Our ideal cannot be the quality of life. That puts comfort, ease, beauty, intelligence, wealth, power and convenience ahead of decency, goodness, kindness and the innate value of every single life created by God. The *quality* of life cannot be more important than the *value* of life. If the quality of life is the prime consideration, who defines quality? Perhaps all the mothers of the mentally deficient will be allowed to obtain a license to do away with any children who cause the family a lower quality of life. If we can hire doctors to abort unborn babies, then the next step may be clinics where we can quite legally murder the elderly or inconvenient. When society accepts convenience and the quality of life as more precious than life itself, the only really valuable people are those who pander to culture's lusts or provide its needs. The thread will break, and wolves will tear the infirm to shreds.

Virtue: Faith and Works

In an adolescent overreaction to "works" righteousness, many modern Christians have an unreasonable fear of any human effort to reach for maturity and wholeness. To be sure, we cannot bring ourselves into right standing with God. Only the blood of Jesus can do that. As Paul writes, "By grace you have been saved, through faith — and this not from yourselves, it is the gift of God — not by works, so that no one can boast" (Eph. 2:8-9, NIV).

And yet Peter urged Christians to add virtue to their faith (see 2 Pet. 1:5).

There is a covenant between the man of God and the God of man which implies life at both ends. Let me give you a parable. Here is a tree, a stone and the sun. The sun rises and says, "Let us make a covenant; I will shine on you, and you respond to me." Can the sun make such a covenant with a stone? Certainly not! The stone has no life; it cannot grow. The stone cannot mature or develop. But what about the tree? Certainly the greater power is with the sun. It is the energy and the influence. The tree, however, can respond to all the sun has to offer. Its response is summoned by the sun, but, unlike the stone, it will twist and reach and thrust to grow in rays of power.

If Western society and the Western church are to survive, it will be because we learn again the simple virtues.

The same thing is true of the Christian. Psalm 37 says, "Trust in him and he will do this: he will make your righteousness shine like the dawn" (vv. 5b-6a, NIV). But we dare not sit like the stone, hardened against the Son of righteousness. In other words, God's willingness to help us must be met with our willingness to be helped. We must add virtue to faith. We must purpose in our hearts for God to teach us true virtue so that it permeates the inner man and becomes the illuminating influence of our lives. In an age of virtueless wolves ranging the land in packs, the man of God must seek illumination. God can teach us virtue, but we must want it. Perhaps a hundred years ago in the West, a book on virtue might have been so obvious as to have seemed frivolous. There would not have been a need to teach or write on virtue. God said the Ninevites did not know their right hand from their left. Perhaps the same might be said of modern America. America has lost her basic concept of virtue.

It is time to demand virtue of ourselves, our courts, our government and our entire society. With our virtue squandered, we are doomed to life on the jungle floor. We must struggle for virtue in our generation.

If Western society and the Western church are to survive, it will be because we learn again the simple virtues. If not, we will sit in numbed silence awaiting the sickening snap when the thread of virtue gives way and our society descends into chaos.

II

COURAGE

The Crucible of Conviction

Ortiz pressed his face against the jagged corner of the building and peered up 83rd Street. The cold wind hit him in the face like a fist. He squinted his eyes in the darkness, straining to watch an old man making his way painfully along the icy sidewalk. Candy from a baby, Ortiz thought, and turned to face his accomplices in the alley behind him. A smile, like a crack in a plaster wall, flashed white teeth in the darkness.

Six pairs of fevered eyes gleamed in the ghoulish blackness of the fetid alley. The level of anticipation rose.

Pulses pounded. Adrenal glands gushed nervous energy in strong, young bodies hot for the hunt.

The kill was imminent. The prey — old, half-crippled, totally defenseless — was staggering right into the gaping mouth of their alley. The little gang crouched, muscles gathering to pounce.

Suddenly, in perfectly practiced timing, Ortiz's hand shot spring-loaded from the alley. The fangs of confusion and fear tore at the old man's throat as Ortiz seized him by his lapels. Then they were on him. Fists and booted feet pummeled the old man into a fog of insensible, confused pain. They circled him, laughing at his pitiful, whimpering gasps.

He was done for. All they had to do was take whatever bits of money he had and leave. But Ortiz had something else in mind. This old piece of trash and his Social Security pocket change were of absolutely no importance to Ortiz.

The eyes of the others were fixed on him. Slowly, deliberately, Ortiz flicked open his switchblade. The horror oozing out of the old man's glazed eyes seemed oddly laughable to Ortiz. Snarling, teeth bared, the boy eased the blade in. The gurgling, abbreviated scream was bitten off by death's steel jaws.

They sauntered out of the alley. There was no hurry. Now, with so much pent-up energy gone, they felt relaxed, fed and ready for more docile pursuits. The youngest of the group, a reedy adolescent with cold blue eyes, hugged his jacket about him and looked back at the wretched corpse.

He asked himself the most important question of his life — of any man's life, he thought. Would he ever be as brave as Ortiz? He doubted himself, and the doubt frightened him. He had feelings that were soft — almost sentimental — about this old man. He had to get that softness out. He was not a woman. He hurried back into the alley where black, putrid death hung in the air. He carefully aimed one swift, brutal kick into the old man's lifeless face. Encouraged, he ran to join his hero and the others. Ortiz seemed far away and high above him, but the memory of the dull thud of his boot against death comforted him.

The snow creaked under their feet as they slowly broke into a nonchalant gallop. They looked so very much like a pack of wolves running in the moonlight that one watching might have expected their leader to stop and bay in fearsome pride. ■

In significant elements of America, courage is comprehended as a total absence of squeamishness at any measure of brutality. Such a concept of courage without regard for law and human decency severs the thread of virtue with shears of real horror.

The way a society comprehends courage will in a great part determine whether it will be a noble civilization or sink into brutality and barbarism.

Courage is *not* the feeling of fearlessness. It is rather that willingness of mind necessary to act out of conviction instead of feeling. One may actually feel quite fearless and act in a cowardly manner. Also, one may feel quite fearful and behave with great courage.

Several years ago the wire services carried an account of a printing press operator in the Midwest, whose employer signed a contract to print a pornographic magazine. This man refused to operate his press on that one contract. He pleaded, "Allow me to work on any other project. Give me the worst hours in the shop. But I won't operate my press when that magazine comes through." He was fired. He appealed to his labor union, which declined to support his "censorship." He lost his job within three years of his pension and retirement.

I discussed this disturbing story with a pastor I know. "What a jerk!" my preacher friend laughed. "Gagging at gnats and swallowing camels. How big of a deal is it? He doesn't have to read them or look at the pictures. That fool hasn't any responsibility in the matter. All he has to do is operate a printing press."

Courage is that willingness to deny my own flesh and do what is noble, regardless of the cost.

That pastor's attitude is indicative of a deep wound in our society. When we can no longer even identify which situations demand truly courageous responses, then we no longer know when to take a stand. Finally we will lose our understanding of what courage is. If a society misdefines courage, it is on the verge of barbarism.

What Is Courage?

Courage is that willingness to deny my own flesh and do what is noble, regardless of the cost. I once counseled a young man and woman who were living together. It was financially expedient for them to do so. They came to me to be married. I counseled them that one or the other of them should move out. I urged that they establish a clean relationship for a full year. I urged them to get married only on the foundation stone of a virtuous relationship.

They explained to me how it would be extremely difficult for them financially. I assured them I knew it would take great courage to be able to act virtuously. They accepted my advice.

30

The expense was not only financial. Their bodies had cultivated an appetite for each other. They were enjoying all the benefits of marriage sexually and none of the responsibilities of the commitment. That is a very difficult thing to reverse, but they did. They acted with tremendous courage, and God blessed them in it.

One of the most satisfying moments of my ministry was receiving a letter from them more than a year later as they honeymooned in Italy.

> Dear Dr. Rutland,
> This is the greatest moment of our lives because we know that we acted as God wanted us to do. Now we have come on this honeymoon together from the foundation stone of a virtuous relationship. If we had gone on living together and gotten married, we would only have been asking the church to solemnize what we were already doing. Now we know that our marriage is founded in Christ. We are so happy.

Merely knowing what is chaste or honest or true is not enough. It takes courage to *act* on virtue. Courage is also the catalytic agent that summons every other virtue into action in the face of temptation or crisis.

A certain contractor agreed to build a house for a certain amount. The contract demanded top-grade materials. A sudden unexpected rise in the cost of that grade of materials caught him and many other contractors by surprise. If he fulfilled the contract as signed, he knew he would lose money.

He also knew he could use a lower grade and get away with it. It probably would not make much difference in the quality of the house. Now the obvious issue was honesty. He knew the honest thing to do, but his honesty would cost him his profit margin. ■

Now it required tremendous courage to act honestly. Honesty is the virtue resident, but it takes courage to put it into action.

Many miss the greater truth of courage by thinking of it solely in terms of bravery. They envision the brave young Allied soldiers who charged the machine guns at Gallipoli in World War I. Though their actions are certainly admirable, courage is far more than valor in the face of danger.

Courage and heroism are not exactly synonymous. Acts of heroism may or may not be indicative of true courage.

Heroism in the face of danger may be a momentary burst of spontaneity not really indicative of character. Certain people are simply constitutionally impetuous. They are bolder than others by nature. Sometimes public heroes in war or athletics later live otherwise unproductive and even destructive lives. Such people were never truly courageous. They were simply heroic.

Imagine two children playing on a swing set. One child, by nature, loves the thrill of danger. "Swing me higher!" she cries. "Push higher, Daddy!"

It may not indicate any great courage on her part. It may rather be that she has a broad thrill spectrum. Her brother, on the other hand, may say, "Not so high, Daddy, not so high." The father may think the lad cowardly. It may be that he is simply more prudent. To confuse prudence and cowardice is dangerous folly indeed.

"Don't be a coward!" is the stinging rebuke the boy gets for his prudence. His heart is damaged needlessly, for he is not cowardly at all. He may, however, be smarter than his sister.

Furthermore, courage without character can degenerate into mere bravado. The distinction between a hero and an obnoxious show-off is defined by character. In other words, if his motives are selfish and impure, the hero's courage may result from a lust for preeminence that overrides good judgment.

Indeed, acts of heroism may sometimes be born of stupidity, ignorance or misunderstanding. For example, the kamikaze pilot in World War II who crashed his airplane directly into the bridge of a foreign ship may, in one sense, be considered courageous. But, realizing he was so misinformed as to have believed his place in the afterlife was thus secured, he proves to be tragically misguided instead of courageous.

> *The distinction between a hero and an obnoxious show-off is defined by character.*

Then, of course, circumstantial reality may be mistaken as courage. A condemned prisoner on death row was offered to select the menu for his last meal. "Mushrooms," he answered. "I want fresh mushrooms. I've wanted them all my life, and I've never tasted them. I've always been afraid I'd get bad ones and be poisoned."

Is Courage Christian?

An important question here presents itself. Is courage, then, a proper Christian virtue? That is to say, does valor have anything to do with goodness? A warrior may fight valiantly, brave all manner of danger, overcome insurmountable odds and defeat a superior enemy, only to plunder the city and outrage its citizenry. Is he courageous? In every classical and biblical sense of virtue the answer is an unqualified no.

Courage and Public Trust

In the inner office and inner soul of every congressman, a nation and a civilization hang in the balance. Until we can cultivate statesmen who are willing to be turned out of office over taking a stand for moral issues, the thread will continue to unravel.

The congressman who violates his conscience for gain blasphemes his office and corrupts his own humanity. Ultimately his character will become so degraded that he will be unable to take a stand. His vote, his influence and his soul will cheapen at every resale. Enthroned as an incumbent, he is elected time and again, until he becomes an empty husk of a politician.

Hardly any endeavor known to man requires more courage than preaching. The man of God preaches what is right regardless of whom it pleases or offends. He not only preaches what is right, but he preaches what is right in a right way.

The policeman who refuses the envelope of money is not only honest; he is courageous. The schoolboy who declines to hear the dirty joke is not just chaste; he is courageous.

Daily Courage

The long, lingering moral crises of life are the most difficult and taxing. The soldier who scurries across twenty yards of open territory in a hail of bullets may simply have acted spontaneously because he used to play this game in his father's backyard. He may have gotten carried away in a burst of adrenalin, but he wins a congressional medal of honor.

Those who stand up day after day under the withering words of their closest friends need far more courage.

A sophomore student athlete at a large university said to me, "I'm through dating. I've had dates with those I thought were the nicest girls on this campus. When I did not make sexual advances to them, they made advances to me. And they were aggressive."

He said, "When some beautiful cheerleader is climbing all over you, begging you for sex, your desires are stirred up. When I refused, they accused me of being a homosexual. Several threatened to tell everyone on campus that I was impotent." Still he refused.

He is a courageous young man. It is far more courageous to live our convictions day after day than to die in battle.

"The next girl I date is going to be a Spirit-filled, blood-washed daughter of Abraham who looks at this thing exactly as I do, or I don't care if I never date again!" he said. "I've made my stand on this issue."

God, give us more like him.

Hail the professional athlete who plays the Superbowl in great pain! It is in a sense a courageous act. However, he may also be driven by base motives such as ego and his share of the purse.

Now compare the athlete with the crippled teenager who wakes up every morning in immeasurable pain. She cannot even go to the bathroom alone. Yet every day she sings praises and goes to her job. Day in and day out, she does what she can do with fingers that rebel and a body that screams in agony. She may never be thought beautiful, never be pursued by men, never know the tender embrace of a loving husband and never bear children. Yet day after day after day, despite her pain, she simply does what is right.

Courage and the Fear of God

Fear is not altogether unwholesome. If a man fears the wrong thing, he will probably not fear the right thing. If he fears the right thing enough, he will not fear the wrong thing at all. All lesser fears will be swallowed up in the life of the man who truly fears God.

Proverbs 29:25 says, "The fear of man bringeth a snare: but whoso putteth his trust in the Lord shall be safe."

The fear of man is a trap. But it is sprung, harmless and baitless, to the man who fears God. The man-fear trap is the leading cause of death in the development of courage. If we fear God more than we fear the good opinion of our mates at work, our spouses, our friends, our congregations, our constituency, or whomever, we are free. If his ultimate fear is the fear of God, what lesser fear can make a man disobey His will or deny His name?

The account of Bruce Olson's capture and ultimate release by South American communist guerillas is stirring. It is a study in quiet, beautiful courage. He did not overpower his guards or use karate or throw hand grenades. He is a missionary, not John Rambo. In confidence born of fearing God more than their bullets, he offered to teach them. Most of them were illiterate. He, being a linguist, was more fluent in their Spanish language than they were. Olson offered to teach them to read and write Spanish. They kept him captive until they learned to read. Then they released him. The fear of the Lord makes us calm, quiet and confident.

Courage and Leadership: Three Kings in Crisis

Styles of leadership, in any era, vary widely, but courageous leaders are at a premium in every generation. Three more disparate kings can hardly be imagined than Herod, David and Jesus. Herod was the quintessential tyrant. He was a collaborator as well as a murderous lecher. But the telling lack in his character was courage.

David was the consummate warrior king. Larger than history, he lived his life in capital letters. When David was good, he was "very, very good, and when he was bad, he was horrid." But at many points in his life we see tremendous courage under extensive pressure.

All lesser fears will be swallowed up in the life of the man who truly fears God.

Jesus, the gentle shepherd, is probably not seen by many as being particularly courageous. He fought no pitched battle, led no troops, scaled no fortress walls. But in His ignoble death by execution, we see courage of the highest order.

Scripture affords us a window into the lives of these three kings. By comparing their performance under the excruciating heat of enormous pressures, we see great, contrasting studies in courageous and cowardly leadership.

I. King Herod

King Herod had stolen his own brother's wife. John the Baptist fearlessly, publicly denounced the king for living in sin with his brother's wife. Herod himself did not even have the gumption to lock the prophet up. He ultimately did it only because his mistress was angry. He was more afraid of his girlfriend than he was of the prophet of God (see Matt. 14:1-4).

> And when he would have put him to death, he feared the multitude, because they counted him [John] as a prophet (Matt. 14:5).

Likewise, when Herod would have executed John, he lacked even the brutal fearlessness to commit murder. Not because he feared God; he feared the people. Fear robbed him of leadership.

> But when Herod's birthday was kept, the daughter of Herodias danced before them, and pleased Herod. Whereupon he promised with an oath to give her whatsoever she would ask. And she, being before instructed of her mother, said, Give me here John Baptist's head in a charger. And the king was sorry: nevertheless for the oath's sake, and them which sat with him at meat, he commanded it to be given her. And he sent, and beheaded John in the prison (Matt. 14:6-10).

Fearful of a treacherous woman, a king killed a prophet. The thread is never so fragile as when leaders are more afraid of men than God. When fearful, blustering, lustful old fools lead nations, the thread is brittle and weak indeed.

II. King David

> And it came to pass, when David and his men were come to Ziklag on the third day, that the

38

Amalekites had invaded the south, and Ziklag, and smitten Ziklag, and burned it with fire; and had taken the women captives, that were therein: they slew not any, either great or small, but carried them away, and went on their way. So David and his men came to the city, and, behold, it was burned with fire; and their wives, and their sons, and their daughters, were taken captives. Then David and the people that were with him lifted up their voice and wept, until they had no more power to weep. And David's two wives were taken captives, Ahinoam the Jezreelitess, and Abigail the wife of Nabal the Carmelite. And David was greatly distressed; for the people spake of stoning him, because the soul of all the people was grieved, every man for his sons and for his daughters: but David encouraged himself in the Lord his God (1 Sam. 30:1-6).

Leadership is a great thing. The courageous man will not shrink from leadership. But when everything goes badly and "Ziklag" is burned; when their wives and children are carried away captive, the people cannot rise up and stone God, with whom they are really angry. Therefore they will rise up to stone their leader. But in the painful loneliness of leadership, unless a man has already developed the ability to "encourage himself in the Lord," he will fail the test.

David learned to encourage himself in God as a mere youth. When a bear came out of the woods to kill his father's sheep, David said, "In the name of the Lord my God, you won't get these sheep!"

He learned to encourage himself in God when all the other shepherds ran off and left the little lambs to the lion.

David alone rose up from his sleeping mat and wrestled the lion to the ground and killed it (see 1 Sam. 17:34-35).

David said, "God is my strength, and God is my refuge" (see Ps. 46:1a). The book of Psalms is not written by a man who never knew fear. It is written by a man who knew deep and abiding fear at times. Yet he had learned in the face of fear to find ultimate courage in his fear of God. He encouraged himself in the Lord his God.

When there is no apparent reason for courage, and God is all that the leader has left, then all he has is everything he needs.

When there is no apparent reason for courage, and God is all that the leader has left, then all he has is everything he needs.

There amidst the smoldering ruins of Ziklag, men turned their stones in their hands and eyed their leader with cold disdain. The future of civilization in Israel hung by the frail thread of the courage of a shepherd-king. And it held.

III. King Jesus

On the night that Jesus was betrayed, His friends were asleep in the grass. His enemies were within earshot across the narrow Kidron Valley. Jesus fell across a stone in a lonely garden and thought of the impending horror of the cross. Not only the physical agony of crucifixion, but the spiritual nightmare of God-forsakenness loomed before Him. Some may say He felt no fear. The Bible says sweat drops like blood splattered on the stone. Fear wrenched in His guts like a knife. Satanic voices screamed in the night. Finally He cried out to God, "O

God, I don't want to do this!" It was only when His soul ached for escape and the air was thick with fear that He uttered his great courageous prayer, "Nevertheless not my will, but thine, be done" (Luke 22:42).

Jesus denied the scream of His own will and the tortured cry of His own flesh and rejected the demand of fear. He acted in magnificent courage. However, He did not awaken His friends, arm them with swords and charge across the Kidron Valley to take the city by storm. That might seem manly and brave, but it would not have been courageous.

His enemies came for Him with their torches bright against the night sky and their swords rattling at their sides. The courageous Savior said, "Here I am; take me and let these go free" (see John 18:8).

Only hours later, a mocking, jeering mob taunted the pitiful "coward" who carried His own cross. Never before had the thread of virtue been so tested. Only Jesus' monumental courage, like a steel cable, held humanity up to God while the demon wolves bayed below.

III

LOYALTY

The Fabric of Community

The pungent smoke of the cooking fire filled the hut with delicious odors. It also stung Uguma's eyes and made him even drowsier from the heavy meal. He felt no need to participate in the discussions of the others. He did not care about matters in this place and only came here to see his brother, who had married into this village.

His head began to nod and jerk. It seemed to him that the others in the little hut were staring at him. Why? The men of the village were naked, just as he was, except for loin cloths. They squatted, elbows on knees, in an almost motionless circle of flesh. Somewhere behind him an old woman cackled. His skin crawled. Something was wrong. What?

Uguma's eyes met his brother's across the fire. Did he see a trace of sadness, or was it fear? Uguma sensed rather than saw a movement behind him. He spun to see a man with a war ax. The heavy blade was suspended for a second, its edge flashing in the firelight.

What a fool he was! He had thought his brother would give him safety in the village. He tried to raise his hands against the blow. It was too late. The gods of this village were very strong and very cruel. He envied a village with such ruthless gods. He hoped his tiny son at home would one day have such gods as these. ■

The seams of community are ripped asunder when treachery becomes an acquired virtue. In a society thus brutalized, no one is safe. Family ties mean little. Friendship means even less. Life without loyalty is fragile in the jungle of Stone Age betrayal.

Loyalty is the very fabric of community. Devoid of basic trust in some kind of mutuality of commitment, relationships cannot prosper. Without loyalty, father and son will live as hated strangers, families will disintegrate and culture will descend to the bestial. Only invented taboos and fearsome superstitions can restrain such a murderous society from utter criminality.

When loyalty is lost, the very fabric of relationship unravels. Even the disloyal man depends on someone else's loyalty. The philandering husband will bitterly resent his accountant's embezzlement. The bribed politician howls over his wife's adultery. The issue is not merely hypocrisy; it is a failure to comprehend the very nature of the virtue of loyalty. No one can translate into relationship a virtue which is fundamentally misunderstood. And no society can expect loyalty to anchor its relationships once treachery becomes admirable.

If loyalty is understood only in terms of isolated relationships, disillusionment and bitterness are inescapable. That is to say, a disloyal man is disloyal in his character rather than in respect to particular relationships.

The prevailing wisdom of contemporary society contends that marital loyalty is irrelevant to job performance.

Quite the contrary! A man is not simply disloyal to his wife — he is disloyal. The wise employer will reason: If he will be disloyal to his wife, why should I expect loyalty?

A disloyal man is disloyal in his character rather than in respect to particular relationships.

J.B. Wise had been the president of Wise Widgets Inc. for four decades. He wondered how many bright-eyed, bushy-tailed young executives he had interviewed, hired or fired in those years. He liked people, and he liked taking these young bucks under his wing and molding them into profitable producers. Widgets had never really fascinated him as much as people.

He had to admit these two applicants were good. Very good! In fact, it grieved him not to hire them both. As the waiter cleared away the last of the dishes, Wise analyzed the eager young hopefuls across from him.

It was strange to J.B. how very much alike they seemed, yet they were so different. Maybe he was just getting so old that all young businessmen in blue suits looked alike. Young Bill Goodman was a tech graduate.

He was knowledgeable, soft-spoken, but slightly book-ish. He definitely yielded the edge to Jim Quisling in charm. Quisling, on the other hand, for all his Ivy League looks, seemed slightly unsure on a few of the more technical points. That, however, was less important to Wise at this stage. You can, he reminded himself with a chuckle, learn widgets. It is hard to learn sales ability. He definitely leaned in the direction of Quisling. Boyish charm can sell plenty of widgets in certain places.

"Do you mind if I ask a question now?" Bill Goodman asked. "My wife advised me to get a clear reading on one point, and I really trust her counsel."

J.B. totally ignored Goodman's question. Instead he seized the moment to test Quisling. "What about you, Jim? Did your wife send you off with any questions in hand?" J.B. tried to allow a convivial condescension to creep into his tone.

"Hardly," Quisling snickered. "She wouldn't know what to ask."

J.B. Wise chuckled conspiratorially and leaned close, hoping to draw Quisling on. "No head for business, eh?"

"No head for much of anything, actually," Quisling answered. "A classic beauty from Boston. But, as they say — the porch light is on, but nobody is home."

The two men shared the joke, but J.B. noticed Goodman sipped his coffee and ignored the jest. He detected no trace of smugness in Goodman's eyes. There was, however, a quiet, unpretentious detachment. He looked like a schoolboy ignoring a smutty joke he didn't really understand anyway.

"And your wife?" J.B. spun to face Goodman, hoping to rattle him. "Does she always tell you what to ask?"

"She certainly doesn't control me, if that's what you mean. But Alice is very bright, and I trust her advice in many areas of life. She's really a wonderful person. I wish you could get to know her."

In that one moment J.B. Wise knew he had his man. Quisling, the Ivy League puffin, had mocked his own wife. What would he say about Wise Widgets in an unguarded moment?

He looked forward to meeting Goodman's wife. ■

The moral and social consequences of venerating the wicked are substantial. Furthermore, doing so is short-sighted beyond words.

The point is, of course, that loyalty is not an issue of trading off. One does not gain six points for voting a straight ticket, then lose three for company disloyalty, finishing at a good solid plus three. Efforts to separate the virtue of loyalty from the social intercourse of life are misguided, at the least, and are usually dangerous. A man does not simply act disloyally in some isolated sense. A man is either loyal or he is not.

Rep. Merritt Smith was a secure, four-term congress-man. Only twenty-four hours ago he seemed invincible. Now he held the front page in his hand like a man holding his own death sentence. "Merritt Smith Indicted!" the headline screamed. The article went on to outline the charges of influence-peddling and money-laundering. To add insult to injury, his secretary, Margaret, had revealed (along with other things) their long-standing affair in a full-color pictorial spread in *Playboy*. He calmed his jangled nerves and massaged his temples. Don't panic! He was sure he could plea-bargain the charges against him down to a misdemeanor and plead *nolo contendre*, taking a reduced punishment. He must show a sad disap-pointment with his own humanity but never admit culpa-bility.

Then, in a fiercely emotional press conference, he

would denounce the newspapers for pouncing on the irrelevant sex scandal. His teary little mouse of a wife would stand bravely at his side while he suffered like a martyr. He played the scene in his mind. "My wife and I have come through this difficult time. She is satisfied about the whole incident, and we are closer now than ever before." At that point he must embrace her protectively. "We believe the voters of this district are sophisticated and intelligent enough to separate these personal matters from my performance in the House of Representatives." He would then boldly announce his candidacy for re-election. Oh, sure, many votes would be lost. But he knew he could count on the evangelical vote. He was "right" on their issues, and Christians love to forgive people. He would be hailed as a hero by many.

This was not going to be fun, but he could make it through. Life goes on, he thought. ■

Stealing Hearts

Loyalty is the willingness, because of relational commitment, to deflect praise, admiration and success onto another. This loyalty may well be at great personal expense, but it will edify and bless its object.

Loyalty never usurps authority. It refuses to accept inappropriate love or praise that might properly exalt another. Loyalty is the glue that holds relationships together, makes families functional and armies victorious. Loyalty is the fabric of society. Without loyalty, no enlisted man can dare to hope that his general cares whether he lives or dies. No captain can expect an inconvenient order to be obeyed. Without loyalty, marriage becomes a competitive minefield. Companies become dangerously paranoid. And ruthless power politics will turn bishops into Machiavellian princes.

Loyalty is the basic element which validates and cements relationships. If husbands are disloyal to their wives, if children are disloyal to their parents, parents to children, employees to employers, then there is no secure relationship, and the fabric of community soon unravels.

Loyalty is the willingness, because of relational commitment, to deflect praise, admiration and success onto another.

Every month, on a certain day, the king's court in Israel was held for people who had exhausted all possibilities of adjudication in civil and criminal matters. On that day anyone could appeal directly to King David. His decisions, just or otherwise, were final. Of course, the backlog of appeals soon became tremendous.

David's son Absalom exploited this frustration for his own advantage. Standing tall in his fine chariot, the strikingly handsome Absalom created quite a stir. As the resplendent chariot rumbled through Jerusalem, Absalom's flowing hair caught the eye of male and female alike. It became his habit to wait at one of the city gates for those coming on the day of the king's court. Flattered at being summoned into Absalom's chariot, men shared openly. He wooed them like a politician. He kissed babies and consoled the hurting, yet offered no hope as long as David ruled.

"It's not altogether David's fault," Absalom would explain sarcastically. "He's overworked. Yet he stubbornly refuses to appoint a deputy. Now if *I* were deputy, I'd make sure you got justice. The appeal ought to go your way, but — well, who knows?"

No one loves a demagogue like the disgruntled. Grateful men bowed down before Absalom and longed for him to be their champion. The crowning blow was Absalom's personal embrace in traditional Middle Eastern style. This was designed to seal their loyalty to Absalom personally. Of course, he had no right to such dedication. Only David had a right to that.

> So Absalom stole the hearts of the men of Israel (2 Sam. 15:6b).

The throne was Absalom's by birth. It should have gone to him. But his untimely and tragic death cost him the throne. Disloyalty is the fertile ground of open rebellion. His disloyalty caused his rebellion, and his rebellion cost him his life. When outward rebellion occurs, it is always because loyalty was not added to faith.

Loyalty refuses to accept inappropriate credit, receive improper admiration or usurp the respect due others. Such loyalty is often cultivated at great personal expense.

Loyalty in Action

Adam Albright is the pastor of a small Midwestern church. He announces to his five adult Sunday school teachers, "God has laid on my heart that for the next three months all of you should teach on evangelism. I've prepared these lesson outlines for you. You can adjust them to suit your classes." The next Sunday, all five begin the series.

Teacher 1 says to his class, "The pastor said we have to teach this stuff for the next three months. I want you to know that if I were the pastor, we wouldn't teach this. But I'm not the pastor, and this lesson isn't mine."

Teacher 2 obediently teaches the material. Her class

responds enthusiastically, becomes soul-winners and actually causes the class and the church to grow. At the end of the series, they sing her praises. "What a great idea you had to teach this series! What great lessons and marvelous outlines you had!"

"Thank you so very much," she says humbly. "I really prayed over it. I knew God was guiding me as I prepared and taught." Obedient in action, she stole the hearts of the people. But it was the pastor's vision, and she should have deflected the praise onto him.

Now *Teacher 3* teaches the series of lessons, but it goes badly. Everyone hates it. The class objects, "We don't want to be soul-winners. We like the easy, comfortable Sunday school class we've had for forty years, and you're pushing us out into the streets. We don't want this."

To this the teacher replies, "It wasn't my idea. I never wanted to teach this stuff in the first place! But you know how the pastor is. Complain to him."

Teacher 4's Sunday school class also complains to her, but she says, "I felt it was what God was telling me to do. I tried to do my best. If the pastor could only have taught it himself, I know he would have done better. So if you're angry, be angry with me." She accepts the brunt of the criticism, allowing all respect and admiration to pass on to higher authority. Furthermore, she probably told the truth; the pastor would have done better.

Teacher 5's class proclaims, "This is the most wonderful thing that's ever happened to our Sunday school class!" To which the teacher replies, "I can agree with you because I had nothing to do with it. God and the pastor worked this out. Pastor wrote it and handed it to me. Frankly, I had my misgivings. But I see now that the pastor was right. I thank God that he gave us this series, don't you?" That is loyalty in action. ■

51

The Strata of Loyalty

A particularly ironic confusion seems to result from our society's general disregard for the virtue of loyalty. We have contracted an inability to prioritize our loyalties. That is to say, confusion in society results from failure to establish appropriate levels of loyalty. Not all loyalties are created equal. Spheres of loyalty will often conflict. Weakness and instability will result in the failure to distinguish levels of loyalty.

We have contracted an inability to prioritize our loyalties.... Not all loyalties are created equal.

Only by working downward from the ultimate level can such contradictions be avoided. By first establishing that loyalty which can never be denied, the tension of crises is eased at descending levels. Once that loyalty among all loyalties is settled, questions of conflict are more easily resolved.

A woman came to me for counseling claiming that her husband was ordering her to engage in prostitution. He was not a Christian, but he knew she was. He made this perverted demand by exploiting two of her convictions. He was head of the household, and she must be loyal to him. She evidently had accepted some kind of strong, legalistic teaching which convinced her that, no matter what her husband said, she had to obey it. This Christian woman was actually considering acceding to his demands.

She was deceived by confused loyalties. By allowing a secondary loyalty, that to her husband, to supersede her ultimate loyalty, her relationship with Jesus Christ, she nearly entered into serious immorality. Her unsaved husband was using her slavish misunderstanding of Scripture to manipulate her into doing what he wanted.

Another woman with whom I once counseled was awaiting her criminal trial for embezzlement. She had gotten involved with a man who was heavily in debt. He had pleaded with her to get some money for him or he would go to prison. She embezzled a substantial amount of money from her job to help him. She fully intended to repay it. The scandal of her arrest was a bitter shock to her church and her family. When I asked how she could have fallen for such a tired old line, she responded that "she had no idea."

She was right! She had no idea. She justified her disloyalty to God with loyalty to a man — and not much of a man, at that.

Our Covenant of Loyalty: Marriage

Second only to an ultimate loyalty to God is loyalty to one's spouse. Marriages are racked by emotional, verbal and sexual disloyalty. Once the wound of disloyalty is opened, only the grace of God can heal it.

My wife and I have counseled with many couples whose marriages have been shaken by extramarital affairs. We try to bring them to the point of being honest with each other about the adultery. We have found that husbands generally ask very different questions at this point than wives do.

Husbands typically ask questions such as, Was he a better lover than I am? Was there something he did for you that I didn't? Did you enjoy him more than me? Wives more frequently ask, Did you talk about me with her? That shocked me the first time a woman asked it. I thought to myself, Of all things that's what you want to know? You want to know what he was talking about? They were sleeping together, and all she's interested in is what they talked about! Slowly I realized why the conversation of the lovers was actually more important to her than their sexual activity. She was not as concerned with the *act* of immorality as she was with what it represented. She sensed that in their conversation she might discern the true depth of the disloyalty.

Loyalty in marriage is quite the same as loyalty in any other relationship. It means constantly building up the other person, even at one's own risk or expense. I cannot imagine a woman being more loyal to her husband than my wife is to me. When I go to preach where my wife has previously spoken, I am often asked, "Are you really as wonderful as your wife says?" Of course, that makes me feel like a million dollars. And I can only very modestly defer to my wife's wisdom and discernment.

Her loyalty then makes me want to respond in kind. It escalates, and we begin to race with each other to see who can build up the other more. For many couples the same process seems to work in reverse.

My wife and I are shocked to hear a couple argue and contradict each other in public.

The husband will say, "I remember back in 1957, we moved to Topeka — "

"No, no, dummy," the wife interrupts. "It was 1956."

"No," he insists, "it was 1957 because it was the year Charlie was born."

"Great!" she cries. "That's typical! It *was* the year that Charlie was born, but he was born in '56. You don't know any of the birthdays of the children."

This tedious conversation goes agonizingly on and on until I imagine myself jumping on the table like the Mad Hatter, stamping about in tea cakes and shouting, "I don't care! I don't care whether it was in '56 or '57. And I don't care about Charlie's birthday!"

Such pathetic arguments are a complete breakdown of marital loyalty. The loyal wife allows her chronically confused husband to state categorically that it was 1957 even if she knows it was actually before the Crimean War. Alone in the car, away from everyone else, she tenderly reminds him, "I know you said 1957, and you're probably right. You almost always are. But it seems to me we were driving a Pierce-Arrow that year. Did we own a Pierce-Arrow as late as '57?"

That affords him a little latitude. If she shouts "1956!" like the volcano goddess, he is going to fight back. It is naive, if not insane, to think he is going to admit in front of five other couples, "Oh, yes, dear, you're right. What a donkey I am."

Husbands, on the other hand, often say the most outrageously disloyal things disguised as jokes. "Are you going to eat *all* of that?" the husband asks as his wife's banana split arrives, borne by two waiters. Her spine rigid with wounded, feminine pride, she announces, "Yes, I'm going to eat this and five more. By Christmas I intend to be as big as the Von Hindenberg."

A certain couple attended a small gathering at our house. They were desperately trying to dig their way out of debt. The woman loudly complained ad nauseum that her husband had taken a second job. The family never saw him. The children were neglected, and she felt like a widow.

My precious wife finally asked the woman to help her in the kitchen for a few minutes. They disappeared for nearly half an hour. When the woman came back, she looked like a naughty child returning to class from the principal's office. For a while she sat quietly. Then, completely out of nowhere, having nothing to do with the conversation, she announced, "You know, that reminds me of what a wonderful man my husband is! Did you know he has taken a second job? He works so hard just to take care of me and the kids."

Alison had helped her realize she was being disloyal to her husband. She was tearing her husband down in front of others, which in turn elevated her stock with no one.

The Disloyalty of Criticism

In criticizing the wisdom and ability of a superior, a subordinate lowers himself. Logic dictates that the lesser works for the greater. Therefore if the boss is the champion nitwit of all time, what kind of people work under him? If the boss is an all-around great person of tremendous insight and wisdom, the happy conclusion is that surely he also had wisdom in his hiring decisions. When I lift up my boss, I am lifted up. When I brag on my wife, I shall be held in honor by others. If I speak of her disloyally, others will agree with me that she certainly is stupid — stupid enough to marry me! Likewise, if my parents are the village idiots — well, they raised me.

Vertical Loyalty: A Two-Way Street

Loyalty must function both upwardly and downwardly. Upward loyalty is shown to our superiors. It is being willing for them to get the credit while we take the blame. This is the key to corporate loyalty. The middle-level employee has both subordinates beneath him and superiors above him. If he exudes any sense of disloyalty, the fabric of community in that corporate structure begins to shred.

A positive example in contemporary American public life is President George Bush. Without endorsing or denouncing his political views, it is nonetheless true that President Bush is where he is today in large part because he learned how to be loyal. As vice president he was willing for President Reagan to get all the glory. There may well have been times when he could have edged into the spotlight or perhaps even done a better job.

The CEO of every corporation should periodically invite someone to teach his employees corporate loyalty. They must know how to deflect praise and admiration onto the boss while at the same time prove willing to accept the blame when things go badly.

In criticizing the wisdom and ability of a superior, a subordinate lowers himself.

I have sometimes had the unfortunate experience of calling someone's office only to have a secretary say, "I don't know where he is. Many times he doesn't even come in until 10 or 11 o'clock. I guess he's playing golf somewhere."

This is blatant disloyalty. The secretary is making her boss look bad. Perhaps it is an attempt to convey that she is there working while the boss plays. She is essentially saying, "I don't know what my boss would do without me."

Upward loyalty helps to fulfill the superior's dreams. Lower-level managers are generally not hired to be visionaries. Any institution must operate on only one vision. An obvious example of this is an ambassador. An ambassador does not get paid to have opinions. Ambassadors get paid to make sure the dreams, visions and purposes of the president and the nation are fulfilled. When a U.S. ambassador presents himself to the court of England, the prime minister cares little about the ambassador's opinions. If he gets them very often, he will surely

call the president and ask, "Who is this guy? I don't want
to hear his opinions, I want to know what *you* think."

Downward Loyalty

Some time ago I went to a certain place of business
owned by a man named John. I was there to meet him and
several others for lunch. We waited for our last arrival out
in John's reception area. With us were John's private
secretary, a receptionist and a junior executive. Finally
the last of our party arrived, quite late. As he rushed into
John's reception area he apologized, "I'm sorry I'm late.
My secretary didn't show up, and everything's crazy at
my office. I'm having a terrible time with my staff."

John, in whose office we stood, said, "I know exactly
how you feel. The worst thing I face is getting good help!"
He said this in front of his own staff! I was so surprised
that I couldn't keep from looking at his employees' faces.
They looked as though they had been slapped. The
younger associate literally slumped. His secretary spun
on her heel, went into her office and closed the door rather
too loudly. The receptionist sat down and started typing
like Lizzie Borden. I searched John's face for some sign
of hostility and found none. I realized that in his insensi-
tivity he had no idea of what he had done.

As soon as John and I were alone, I said, "Brother, do
you realize you just lacerated three of your employees?
You badly hurt your own stock with these people." He
seemed genuinely surprised, but when I rehearsed the
scenario for him, the light gradually dawned. I said,
"Think about how you would feel if that had happened to
you. Your employees felt betrayed. You were disloyal to
them. Furthermore, you missed a golden opportunity to
solidify their loyalty to you."

Downward loyalty is people at the top saying, "I

couldn't get this done without these people."

Bosses should constantly be saying, "Any success I have is because of my secretary and associates." They should be praising their employees, not just to their faces, but to other people.

In Army Officer's Candidate School, loyalty is among the first lessons. The army teaches that the superior officer should never mention his rank, and the junior officer should never forget it. If the general constantly complains about his "stupid colonels and incompetent majors," his attitude is disloyal. His staff will not only be disloyal to him, they may tamper with his brakes.

Downward loyalty is people at the top saying, "I couldn't get this done without these people."

The Supernatural Power of Loyalty

The redemptive grace of loyalty is so powerful it can literally infuse any situation with healing and miraculous blessings. Any force that powerful, however, cannot be violated without dire consequences. There are few virtues in the kingdom more honored by God than loyalty. David's loyalty to an unworthy Saul confirmed his destiny for the throne.

Absalom's disloyalty to David sealed his doom.

In the household of Naaman, a Syrian general, there lived a young Jewish slave girl. She had been captured by a Syrian raiding party. Plucked from the bosom of her family, alone in a foreign land, she served as a personal body slave to Naaman's wife — hardly a circumstance to inspire loyalty. Even the most obedient slave might well

59

murder his master mentally. Yet this little girl chose to be loyal from her heart. Somehow her family in Israel had deeply instilled the virtue in her during her childhood. Now, under duress, she cultivated an attitude of humble, loving concern. Strangely, this loyal concern was for the one who owned her just as he owned his horse.

When Naaman contracted leprosy, the slave girl told her mistress, "Would God my lord were with the prophet [Elisha] that is in Samaria! for he would recover him of his leprosy" (2 Kin. 5:3).

Amazing! She sent him who held her captive to her home country, where she surely longed to be. She sent him to be set free of his disease, though he held her in slavery. And indeed he was healed. The miracle which Naaman received was by the ministry of Elisha. But it would never have happened without the slave girl's unlikely loyalty.

Elisha's servant and understudy was Gehazi. This man was in training under Elisha, just as Elisha had served Elijah. Gehazi shook his head in amazement when Elisha declined the munificent rewards proffered by Naaman. The Syrian had been miraculously healed! Why shouldn't Elisha be blessed? Gehazi reasoned in his heart.

But, no! This hard prophet refused the luxurious gifts of the Syrian. Gehazi waited until Naaman was out of Elisha's sight, then raced after the foreign general.

Elisha had changed his mind, Gehazi explained to the Syrian. Two visiting prophets had arrived, and Elisha would now be happy to accept some gifts after all. Certainly Naaman was happy to give.

Elisha, however, discerned the deception and struck the hapless Gehazi with leprosy. In other words, if Gehazi wanted the Syrian's money, then by all means he should have his disease as well.

The greed of Gehazi is obvious. The subtler issue of

his disloyalty is more easily overlooked. For personal gain he misrepresented his employer's motives. Acting out of self-interest, he denied his superior's nobility, goals, purpose and will.

The little slave girl's miraculous loyalty brought healing and blessing; Gehazi's disloyalty brought scandal, disease and death. Loyalty is a gemstone virtue whose luster, in a golden setting of faithfulness, brings glory to God and health to all it touches.

IV

DILIGENCE

The Priority of Perseverance

Mountain High School's battered old Blue Bird bus was symbolic of the track team it carried. The ancient vehicle seemed to be held together with wire. It was not pretty, and it looked like a relic from another era, but it ran fairly well and got where it was supposed to go.

Bouncing along on the torn green seats inside, the little team attempted in vain to act confident and relaxed. On the front seat, gruff old Coach Hardeman pretended to be dozing. His hat was shoved forward over his eyes, and his arms were folded across his chest. Mr. Wheelwright, the good-natured school janitor who doubled as the bus driver and campus Grandpa, whistled the same nondescript tune he had been whistling for years.

The boys were mostly quiet except for the occasional outburst when a spit-wad SCUD found its mark or when some halfhearted insult earned reaction. They were intimidated. In fact, they were terrified. Never in Mountain High's inglorious athletic history had any of its teams made it to the state meet. Many of the boys had never seen Lexington. Blue Rock, Kentucky, seemed insignificant to them as they stared out at the huge city. It made them feel insignificant as well. Despite the forced joviality, several wished they had not come.

Suddenly Coach Hardeman sat up straight, pushed back his hat and stretched his arms above his head. Spinning to face the boys, he stared down the length of the shabby old bus. He searched the face of each of his skinny charges.

"This here's a big city, ain't it?" he asked.

The boys muttered their assent, staring vacantly out the windows.

"I don't reckon we gonna win every event," he continued. "But no school in the state is gonna win 'em all. The main thing is — you're here! This is an invitational, and you were all invited. You deserve to be here."

"We'll do our best, coach," Donny Raffield shouted.

"Yeah, I know you will." The coach smiled as he spoke.

"Coach, what about the long-distance race?" Harold Wilson asked. "Craig Butterworth's home with the mumps." This last comment, which was a fact everyone knew, brought forth a burst of laughter.

"I'm glad you asked that, Harold, because I have a surprise for everyone. Beau Rogers is going to run it."

All eyes turned to the face of the senior water boy. Year after year Beau went out for the track team only to be made the manager. Beau grinned sheepishly from the back seat and shrugged his shoulders.

"But, coach," Cass Davies objected.

"No buts! All of you have your own events. I asked him, and he agreed. That's that." Coach set his lips in a firm line.

From the back, somebody muttered, "He can't win. Heck, he can't even place high."

"I didn't ask him to win or place high. I only asked him to finish," Coach answered as little Beau Rogers, water boy, turned to gaze without expression at the passing traffic.

"I didn't ask him to win or place high. I only asked him to finish."

The day went pretty much as expected. Mountain High placed third in the 100-yard dash and fourth in the 440 relay. That was it. As they began repacking their gear, they heard the top-ten finishers in the long distance race being announced as they crossed the line.

Out of a statewide field of one hundred runners, finishing tenth was an accomplishment. But Beau Rogers's name was not among the ten.

The lights began to dim as the last of the spectators drifted toward the parking lot. The Mountain High boys stared in confusion at Coach Hardeman. He was gesturing madly at the head official. The two men's voices were loud, nearly to shouting, but the boys could not hear the words. The rugged mob of Appalachian teens drifted closer to the argument.

"All right!" they heard the official shout. "We'll turn the lights back on. But it makes no sense. The track meet's over. Just call him in."

65

"No," Hardeman said. "I told him to finish. Let him finish."

"All right, all right," the official muttered. "Turn 'em on," he shouted up to the control tower by the press box. "Turn the lights back on!"

Only when the stadium lights came back to full power did they see him. Struggling around the far turn was Beau Rogers. His arms dangled limply at his sides. His frail legs barely moved. The boy's head wobbled pitiably.

They stared at him in incredulity. The return of lights drew the attention of the few remaining spectators loitering at the gates, and they began drifting back toward the infield. The lone figure laboring up the cinder track moved toward the finish line in obvious agony. Gasping for breath, the boy struggled with each step.

As the cluster of spectators grew, the Mountain High track team became aware of the comments of the adults around them.

"Look at that."

"Why doesn't he quit?"

"I never saw anything like it."

Suddenly somebody cheered. More cheers. Oblivious to the rising cheers, Beau Rogers tried to concentrate on nothing but the finish line. His legs were screaming in pain. He knew he was close to vomiting. Still he came. Right. Left. Right. Left.

He collapsed across the finish line and into his coach's arms. The team swarmed around him, shouting and jumping on him as if he had just won an Olympic gold medal. As the boy lay back against Coach Hardeman's arm, he became aware of the excitement around him.

"What are they cheering about, coach?" he whispered.

"They're cheering for you, son. They're cheering you."

It made no sense to the boy. What did it mean?

66

"I finished, coach, just like you said," he answered.
"Yeah, Beau, that's right. ■

It is a perverse society indeed which lauds its occasional genius and scorns the diligent. How strange that we so honor the gifted, who are what they are without effort or sacrifice. What honor is due them?

Western civilization has placed a premium on talent while quaint relics like diligence gather dust in the moral flea markets of our age.

In so doing we cultivate characterlessness. The modern American sees work as the curse of the gods upon the heads of masses. The faithful, diligent journeyman is mocked as an unimaginative peon unworthy to be in the same room with the fey royalty of creative genius — even if that genius is corrupt, base, unproductive and undisciplined.

As a result, the economic community of the West is indeed hanging by a thread. Hard work and discipline go unrewarded while unmanageable "geniuses" are elevated.

American industry is rapidly gaining a reputation for creative ideas that will not work and a lazy, undisciplined work force that cannot produce. The American work force is confused by its own mythology. We have been taught that, despite our slipshod methods, disregard for diligence and short-run, quick-fix tactics, American ingenuity would somehow make it all come together at the last minute.

We stare disillusioned at vehicles which won't run, banks that fail, ministries that do not last and factories that must be closed. In the 1950s, American industry laughed at pitiful Japanese efforts to mimic Western innovations. But with classical Oriental diligence they have seized the high ground. Creative research and development, they said, will come. First, they maintained, we must work. They proved to be true what we once knew. Genius is a fragile and pitiful substitute for virtue.

Likewise, American education has squandered its soul and its power in a philosophical vanity fair. We are now reaping the bitter harvest of a generation of fanciful but quite useless rhetoric. Our schools and universities continue to spew out graduates who can explain the peyote cult and do African folk dances but cannot hold down jobs.

Diligence is the virtue that sets us free to fulfill our creative destiny.

The university campus, we are told by undisciplined dilettantes, is to be the marketplace of ideas. What about the idea that diligence is not the last resort of the boring and unimaginative? Diligence is the virtue which leads on to balanced, successful living and creativity unfettered by dissipation and decadence.

Stories such as the one about the tortoise and the hare must look like laughable antiques to the modern student. The diligent tortoise now plays comic straight man in an educational system which celebrates the madcap talent of the hare and blames his ultimate failure on a society unable to accept a genius ahead of his time.

When a class is studying Edgar Allan Poe's brooding prose, why not teach the young to learn from his destruction and get a heart of wisdom? In addition to revelling in Poe's works, we must lament the unwritten stories washed away by booze. Instead of producing young musicians who have merely mastered Mozart's concertos, can we no longer marry virtue to genius so as to defeat Mozart's demons? The genius of Mozart must be recognized. His idiotic waste should be a warning to the wise to turn aside and get wisdom. While studying the art of Van Gogh, we must dare to contemplate masterpieces never painted because of mental disease and dissipation. Diligence is the virtue that sets us free to fulfill our creative destiny.

Diligence as Steady Application

Steady application may not necessarily elevate the peaks of the super performer, but it can put a foundation under him to minimize the contrast of his valleys. Furthermore, it enables "Steady Freddy" to reach his potential. The diligent man is a steady performer, and the steady performer is a *finisher*.

One of the most frequent weaknesses among youthful Christians today is a will-o'-the-wisp lightheartedness about obligations. It is not uncommon for an otherwise serious young Christian to testify glowingly, "I was supposed to go to work tonight, but I just felt the Holy Spirit telling me to be here at Bible study." He did not hear that from the Holy Ghost. Don't blame that irresponsibility on God. Such a Christian was informed by his own deceitful heart that it was more fun to sit with his girlfriend at Bible study than to bag groceries.

Well-meaning young zealots occasionally say to me, "I am called to missions, and I know I'm supposed to give two weeks' notice. I also owe some money, and my dad co-signed on my car. But God is telling me to go into the mission field — right now!"

No, He is not! God is calling all of us to be diligent, faithful finishers. If we cannot be trusted to pay our debts, how can He trust us to save Africa?

For good or ill, we always impact with our own character those things committed to us. As we are shaped in the image of Christ, those areas over which we have authority will also bear the stamp of His character.

Diligence as Immediate Obedience

Diligence not only finishes the job, it does so without unnecessary delay. Paul called it "being instant" (2 Tim. 4:2).

It is a Christian virtue to do it now. Procrastination is not merely an inborn personality weakness. Procrastination is a sin and a sign of spiritual backsliding. The diligent man has disciplined himself to hear from the authority in his life and to obey now. Therefore, when God speaks, the diligent man is able to hear from God and obey now. We must teach our children that if they cannot obey parents whom they can see, they will never learn to obey God, whom they cannot see.

The free-thinking lone wolf is so celebrated that exact obedience is often mocked.

There is another even more ominous danger in procrastination. As we procrastinate, we begin to believe that God also is a procrastinator. But the Word of God teaches that God is faithful and He will execute judgment in His time. When that happens, it will come suddenly. The downward cycle of life in a society without diligence is grim. Because authority is not diligent to punish, lack of diligence is learned. A generation with no fear of authority becomes less diligent. Indolence and idleness breed sin and rebellion. Still authority will not be diligent to punish. To such a people, the wrath of God seems unrealistic, if not laughable.

Diligence as Exactitude

Ezra 7:23 says, "Whatsoever is commanded by the God of heaven, let it be diligently [exactly, NAB] done for the house of the God of heaven: for why should there be wrath against the realm of the king and his sons?"

In other words, do it now, do it exactly as instructed and do it until it is finished. America's romance with creative individualism has often worked to a disadvantage in this regard. The free-thinking lone wolf is so celebrated that exact obedience is often mocked.

I took a certain young man on a mission trip to Peru some years ago. We were going into the Amazon jungle to Puerto Bermudez. I had been there many times and knew the journey well. By rented car we would go from Lima to La Oroya to Tarma to La Merced. It would be a long, cold, dangerous night's journey. From La Merced, by an ancient bus, we would travel right down into the jungle to Puerto Bermudez. I knew it would take more than twenty-five hours from Lima. It is a frightening, excruciatingly tedious journey. I knew we would arrive at a lonely jungle army garrison at about three in the morning. I did not think I had to explain to my companion, a young man in his twenties, all the reasons for my instructions.

I simply said, "Now look — put your passport in your shirt pocket. Keep it there, and put everything else in your suitcase."

When we arrived at the military checkpoint at three o'clock in the morning, everyone was nervous and irritable. Peru is an immensely dangerous place. People are being killed every day. The soldiers are nervous. The people are nervous. There is nothing scarier than ten or twenty nervous, tired soldiers manning a jungle outpost at three o'clock in the morning. They are scared of you.

You are scared of them. The whole situation is nerve-racking.

When we jolted to a stop, I awakened my young friend. "Come on," I said. "Get out of the bus."

Everyone on the bus shuffled into line in front of a captain seated at a desk. Sleepy soldiers guarded the line with machine guns. The captain began checking and stamping travel documents.

"What are they doing here?" asked the boy.

"They're going to stamp our passports. Get yours out," I said.

"Passport?" he asked, with horror in his voice. "It's in my suitcase."

"In your suitcase?" I demanded. "Do you mean the one tied on the top of the bus, underneath that goat?"

"Yes," he whined, "up there."

I calmly explained the situation to him. "In a minute that man over there will demand to see your passport. When you fail to produce one, those soldiers will point those machine guns at you. At that time I'm going to step away from you."

He begged pitifully, "Dr. Rutland, please."

"I told you to put your passport in your pocket," I said.

Then he said those hated words. "But I thought...," he moaned. "I thought it would be safer up there."

"Yes," I said, "but you did *not* do what you were told. Now *you* would be safer up there."

At that very moment the sullen captain muttered, "Pasaporte." His voice shaking, my young friend said, "I don't have it," and began gesturing at the decrepit bus. When I saw three Uzis trained on him, I quickly stepped away.

We had to get the goats off the roof of the bus. We had to drag the suitcase down. We had to go through it all till we found his passport. Everybody on the bus was angry at us. They were literally cursing us. Finally we had to repack his suitcase, lift it back on the top of the bus and replace the goats. When we finally rolled out of the outpost, it was five o'clock in the morning. It should have taken us fifteen minutes. It took nearly two hours. The soldiers were angry. The people were angry. I was angry. Why? Because of three fatal words: "But I thought...."

Ingenuity has its place. But the greater virtue is diligence, in this case coupled with obedience.

Partial obedience is disobedience. Delayed obedience is disobedience.

One concept which young Christians have difficulty grasping is that doing a secular job well and exactly as told has an enduring spiritual impact. There is a connection between the way I do my job or clean my room and my relationship with God. If I do the things required of me in a resentful and rebellious manner, diligence cannot be part of any task. When anybody learns that diligence does not matter, his inner spirit suffers.

Negative spiritual lessons are learned when obedience and diligence are unimportant. God may call on the man with diligence and prove him unfit. He may delay. He may do it halfway. He may improvise. He may fail! Partial obedience is disobedience. Delayed obedience is disobedience.

Do it promptly. Do it exactly as told. Finish it.

Diligence as Carefulness

To be diligent also means to use care. For example, the young stock clerk is told, "Stack these five boxes." He may do it quickly and complete the task, yet fail utterly by breaking everything in the boxes.

In this sense, diligence has to do with attitude as well as action. We must do every job as unto the Lord. I must make my job as important to me as it is to my employer, or I sin against him.

Throughout the time I was in college, my wife and I worked hard to hold body and soul together. I often worked at two or three jobs doing whatever I could do to raise the next semester's tuition. At one job in a local grocery store, there were also two other guys who worked there. One was a hotshot local basketball star. His coach had arranged for him to get the job there in order to pick up some spending money. He thought it was a lark, so he played at the job. The other fellow was a slightly retarded young man. The basketball player constantly made him the butt of every joke. Yet I learned by watching that mentally retarded boy bag groceries. Whether there was one person or fifty persons in line, he never altered his course. He would carefully place one can at a time in the sack, not allowing pressure to force him into error. He never hurried. He never got flustered. He never tried to move faster than he could do the job efficiently.

The basketball player was six-foot-nine and marvelously coordinated. When he wanted to, he could bag groceries like a whirlwind. With one hand he could bag groceries faster than the mentally retarded young man could with both hands at top speed. But then the athlete would start clowning or be in the back taking a break when he was supposed to be bagging groceries. Or he would smart off to the boss. I have never been so gratified in my entire life as on the day the manager fired that basketball star. He fired him right in front of the retarded boy. I will never forget that manager pointing his finger at the retarded boy and shouting, "You see this kid? You don't think much of him, do you? He is worth his weight in gold. And you're not worth a dime."

I learned a lesson right there. Just be the best you can be. Just put the groceries in the bag one can at a time. Just finish. Just do it right. Just do it with care. That retarded boy cared about the job. He wanted to do it right. He felt a responsibility to the grocery store. He handled a can of tomatoes as if it were a live baby. The basketball player dropped crates and burst open boxes. He deserved to be fired.

Diligence is also important in relationships. We must be aware of what is going on around us and be sensitive to others. The husband who forgets his wife's birthday is not simply stupid. He is not diligent before God. An apology the day after her birthday is not worth a hill of beans.

Diligence means being sensitive to others and aware of what is going on. Why do American teens feel so little spontaneous impulse to help? A mother can be carrying in two bags of groceries and a gallon of milk. As she struggles with the door, she calls out, "Somebody come and help me." Her great big teenage boy will casually get up off the couch, lay the funny papers aside and graciously hold the door for her. It is because he has never been taught to open his eyes and look at her. He does not really see what she is doing.

The diligent who learn to be observant of others seldom have to apologize later for being thoughtless.

Diligence as a Spiritual Issue

If we fail to learn diligent observation, we may well miss God in important situations. There is something arrogant about spoiled ministers who do not seek to be aware of what God is doing. Such failure even to attempt to be spiritually alert to the situation is sinful and self-indulgent. They are asleep at their posts. They are not prayed up, awake to the Spirit or diligent in the Word. Therefore they cannot, with any confidence at all, say, "Thus saith the Lord." Spiritual diligence — to hear and obey God — is one absolutely essential ingredient in a ministry of genuine power.

Observant in Business

Diligence then means to be on guard, careful, watching over the situation as if it were your own. It means to limit disruptions and distractions.

Secretaries can pay attention to each other or they can be attentive to duty, to their employer and to the situation. The diligent learn to sort through information and see what is worthy of attention. Those clustering around the proverbial water cooler are neither discerning nor diligent. There is some information that is totally useless. Listen with discernment, and limit time spent on useless information.

Diligence and Temptation

The diligent Christian will also be stronger in the face of those surprise temptations which arise suddenly to defeat so many. Everyone will be caught unaware from time to time. But those who are diligent in the things of the world tend toward diligence in the things of the Spirit. The lion is not nearly so able to leap out from hiding and destroy the diligent with an unexpected temptation.

Recently I counseled a young man whose girlfriend was pregnant. He said, "We never intended this to happen."

I don't believe he said that to me. I wanted to say sarcastically, "Well, no, son. Of course you never intended it! Do you think I'm an idiot?"

They allowed themselves to be caught in a situation where they failed morally. Through lack of diligence, sin became almost inevitable. Biology is a tremendous force. We must teach our teens to respect its power.

We often drift into sin because of simply not being observant.

You may be a sanctified, holy, tongues-talking, love-Jesus-with-your-whole-heart Christian who reads the Bible and prays every day. But if you get in the back seat of a car and neck passionately for an hour and forty-five minutes, you are probably going to make love. At some point in all that awakened passion your ability to make a decision to stop will be gone. Once you pass that point of no return, sin is inevitable. Look ahead at the situation. Be observant to possible danger and avoid it.

I have been all around the world and seen all kinds of things. I have never heard of anybody getting pregnant in a prayer meeting. We often drift into sin because of simply not being observant. Round and round the mulberry bush, the monkey chased the weasel. The monkey thought it was all in fun. Pop goes the weasel! A diligent monkey does not chase dangerous weasels. He is alert to the danger in the situation.

Diligence: Key to Growth

None of this is to glorify self-will. Self-discipline is not a way to sanctify ourselves. God must do that. But we cannot go on worshipping our own bellies in self-indulgent, lackadaisical Christianity while praying to God to add virtue to our lives. God expects *us* to discipline ourselves.

A.W. Tozer said, "We have been snared in the coils of spurious logic which insists that if we have found God, we need no more seek Him."[1] Only by having met the Lord can we realize what it really means to seek His face diligently.

Diligence is a key to prosperous, successful living in temporal matters, but God uses temporal concerns to teach us spiritual lessons.

What Diligence Is Not

Diligence is not driven, anxiety-ridden, burdened perfectionism. That neurotic life-style finally becomes temporary and counterproductive. Diligence is productive and enduring. The driven, perfectionistic workaholic is always unable to reach his own unattainable standards, is obsessed but not controlled. He loses his awareness of reality and of the people around him. His wife, children and the real circumstance of his own health and limitations are ignored. He is neither prudent nor cautious. He thinks he is diligent about work, but he actually has his nose buried in his own obsession. Do not confuse that with diligence.

Diligence in Summary

The virtue of diligence has four faces:
- Diligence means *constancy*. Temporary obedience is disobedience.
- Diligence is *instant*. Delayed obedience is disobedience.
- Diligence is *exactitude*. Partial obedience is disobedience.
- Diligence is *observant care*. Careless obedience is disobedience.

Diligence is the responsible, orderly, steady application of God's power within me toward whatever responsibility is mine.

Diligence and Commitment

The Latin form of the word "diligence" is *diligentia*. It derives from two root words which mean "to choose" and "to love earnestly." The diligent man, therefore, is a man who can make and be faithful to a choice, even one that is contrary to the immediate demands of his own flesh.

In marriage, therefore, the diligent man is the man who knows that true love transcends the emotional rush of the honeymoon. Love is a constant choosing. The diligent love earnestly because they choose to love, and they choose to love no matter what. There is a dreadful fragility in any marriage which depends on love being "felt." There are going to come those moments in marriage, or in any relationship, when honeymoon romance is nowhere to be found. That is when we must love not passionately but earnestly, because we choose to do so.

Diligence makes all of life a labor of love, all the way to the finish line.

V

MODESTY

The Fashion of Simplicity

The early Christian community was Jewish. Its struggle was not to know how to live a holy life. Since remotest antiquity, the Law of Moses had prescribed the tiniest details of family, business and social life. The struggle for these Jewish Christians was to comprehend salvation by faith in the gracious Messiah.

As they met there on Solomon's porch, those early Messianic Jews were not seeking a radical change in life-style. They were celebrating the love and liberty of the Holy Spirit while awaiting the return of the King.

However, Jesus delayed His return, and Jewish Christianity was forced out of the temple, out of Jerusalem and finally out of Israel. Gradually the Christian movement began to puncture the soft underbelly of the Greco-Roman world. The insularity of Jerusalem hardly prepared them for the jaded decadence of the decaying remnants of imperial glory. Rome had become a tired old whore whose depraved appetites corrupted not only its flamboyant royalty, but the general population as well. Dry rot had reached the courts, families, theaters and businesses of the common man.

Style of dress is an application of modesty, not a definition.

In the blazing revivalism of Ephesus (Acts 19), the impact of Christianity was an immediate change in life-style. Huge collections of magic books and paraphernalia were burned.

The Ephesians were idolatrous gentiles, not legalistic Jews. Their idols, mostly of the goddess Diana, were destroyed, and they refused to purchase more. The silversmiths who made the statues knew that this new life-style for the Christians meant an end to their industry, and riot resulted.

In Jerusalem, however, no bonfires of the Torah were burnt. There was no particular industry which depended upon pervasive sin. Christianity was a theological issue in Jerusalem. In Ephesus and Corinth and Rome itself, the issue was how to live as a Christian in the putrid atmosphere of decaying paganism.

Christians in Jerusalem in 33 A.D. were asking, "When will He come again, and what will the restoration of David's kingdom look like?"

Christians at Ephesus less than thirty years later were

asking a different set of questions. How do we do business? Should we buy meat dedicated to pagan gods before being sold? How should we treat slaves? How should our women dress?

By the late nineteenth and early twentieth centuries, Western civilization had been pretty thoroughly Christianized. Certainly that does not mean everyone was a Christian. It means rather that mores, values and ways of living were profoundly informed by Christianity.

Not everyone was honest, but there was a societal consensus about what honesty was. Not everyone went to church, but going to church was considered a "good" thing to do. And not everyone was modest, but modesty was considered a virtue.

That's not necessarily true anymore. Modesty is now more often considered the neurotic repression of both sexuality and individuality. In fact, many will reason that if America is about individual liberty, modesty may actually be "bad."

Part of the problem the church faces today is that, in addition to being misunderstood, modesty has often been applied narrowly by the church itself.

Now we are in the post-Christian era of the West. The moral decay around us is forcing Christians to come up with answers which are no longer "givens." Fending off the old legalism of Jerusalem on the one hand, we must also resist libertine corruption on the other.

Living Within Limits

Most modern Americans see the word "modesty" as applying only to one's manner of dress, and even then it is mostly used with regard to women. Yet modesty actually has far more to do with self-respect and self-control than with how revealing one's garments are. Style of dress is an application of modesty, not a definition.

Modesty, in its classical sense, means living within limits. Modesty submits to the boundaries of propriety. It is the opposite of being "bold-eyed," putting oneself forward in the sense of being overly aggressive or presumptuous. Modesty has to do with being other than boastful and arrogant.

Modesty springs from a tempered and humble estimation of one's own importance. It is unobtrusive, but it is not bashful. Modesty acknowledges the fact that there are limits of propriety on my life and that it is good to submit to those. Modesty sees those restraints as being positive safeguards, not negative hindrances.

Immodesty denies responsibility to law, culture, authority and tradition. Immodesty is personally offended by signs that say Stay Off the Grass. Modesty says, There are things in this world that are right for me to do, and things in this world that are not right for me to do. And I am not too good or too big or too rich or too powerful for someone else to point those out to me.

Modesty is not mindless subjection to authoritarianism. It is rather the conviction that there are correct limits on my life. In addition, the modest learn to set their own limits. Modesty has a great deal to do with one's self-view.

There is a great insight on modesty in Romans 12:1-3:

> I beseech you therefore, brethren, by the mercies of God, that ye present your bodies a living sacrifice, holy, acceptable unto God, which is your reasonable service. And be not conformed to this world: but be ye transformed by the renewing of your mind, that ye may prove what is that good, and acceptable, and perfect, will of God. For I say, through the

grace given unto me, to every man that is among you, not to think of himself more highly than he ought to think....

That is the essence of modesty. That passage was written to help pagans in Rome — and America — to understand that modesty means much more than how a woman dresses.

Paul says, "I beseech you therefore, brethren,...that ye present your bodies a living sacrifice, holy, acceptable unto God..." (Rom. 12:1). Obviously, then, we are precious. We are important to God. Otherwise the sacrifice of our lives would be totally unacceptable to Him. If your body is a sacrifice which is acceptable to God, then treating your body with respect is also important to God.

Modesty, in its classical sense, means living within limits.

Verse 3 says, "Don't think more highly of yourself than you ought to think." That is, a sacrifice is acceptable to God only as long as it is on the altar. When it is presented unto God, it finds its meaning. Withdrawn from the altar of God and claimed for itself in arrogant, presumptuous self-ownership, your body loses its meaning and therefore its value.

Hence, in being yielded as a sacrifice under the ownership and lordship of Jesus Christ, I find meaning and explanation. But when I take my body and my life in my own hands, I make myself meaningless and valueless. Then my life becomes an unending search for ways to convince myself and the world of my significance.

Modesty is unassuming and genuinely humble. The immodest announce by demeanor, dress and attitude, to everyone in general and to the opposite sex in particular,

"Look at me. I am what is important in this place."

As she passed the full-length mirror, Kristy Peterson checked herself out. She was transfixed by what she saw. She was very pretty, if not actually beautiful. Even better than beautiful, however, Kristy was rich and beautiful.

Her hair was exactly as she wanted it, though she complained about it constantly. Her sweater-shirt was obviously expensive and fashionable. The top two buttons were open, and the braided gold chain which delicately graced her smooth neck lay across her upper chest. From the chain dangled a seven-hundred-dollar cross with a beautiful little diamond. Her father had complained that it was too expensive for a teenager's necklace, but her mother had successfully interceded as usual. After all, a girl's sixteenth birthday comes only once. It wasn't as if her father could not afford it.

Kristy opened the sweater's third button, revealing a shapely figure. The teenager knotted her brow, wrinkled her nose and pursed her lips in the cute pout with which she consistently charmed most males and many females. She rebuttoned the sweater, pouted again and finally unbuttoned it yet again and pulled the sides open just a tiny bit more.

The cross looked absolutely tantalizing on her upper chest. There, that was better. Anyway, the cross should show. It was a birthday present. After all, it *was* a cross, and everybody in town knew her family was very prominent at First Church. She was not ashamed of that. She tossed her head, corrected her posture and swirled from the mirror, out of the girls' bathroom and into the lonely hall.

A few quick strides later Kristy stood at the door of the yearbook office. The rest of the committee was inside. She knew they had already been working for three quarters of an hour and were likely to be unreasonable with her. She would fix that. With her hand on the doorknob, she carefully arranged her most dazzling smile, absolutely confident of its effect.

She threw open the door and danced in, nonchalantly tossing her purse onto a nearby desk.

"Sorry I'm late," she sang out to the room in general.

"What else is new?" answered Carl "the Nerd" Stanton.

She flashed him her most wounded look but said nothing, waiting for others to try to make her feel better. They did not. Instead, the six other teenagers continued their work with hardly a notice of her presence.

"Hi, Kristy," said Elizabeth Benton, the yearbook editor. A chorus of half a dozen "hellos" followed, but they were shockingly halfhearted. Kristy seethed at being so blatantly ignored. Were they trying to punish her for being late?

"Well, I see I'm not needed," Kristy muttered petulantly.

"Sure you are," Elizabeth said patiently. "There's enough work for all of us. Why not trim those pictures on that desk?"

"OK," Kristy answered quietly. She really did not like Elizabeth Benton. Elizabeth was pretty in a way, but she just did so little with herself. Elizabeth was what Kristy's father called a "real little lady." The phrase made Kristy sick. But she felt she should be seen with Elizabeth occasionally. The Benton girl was well-liked and extremely smart.

Kristy ambled over to the desk littered with pictures, sat down and listlessly began the required trimming. She had learned over the years that being barefooted in a room full of people with shoes on always got attention. She thought it made her look free and uninhibited. She lifted both feet and let her pumps drop to the tile floor with a very satisfying clatter. At the noise, several boys glanced at Kristy. Now Kristy studiously ignored *them*.

She propped her feet on a chair and lounged backward, pretending to be absorbed in the scissor work. She knew she was finally starting to get some attention. Sitting like that with her feet up, more of her legs would be exposed. Well, who cares? She was just being herself. Could she help it if they looked?

Kristy knew her father would not have liked it. If he could see her now, he would fume just as he did whenever she wore shorts to night church. He was sweet, but he was also completely out of it, she thought.

In a few minutes three of the boys were at her desk, and Elizabeth Benton, Carl "the Nerd" and that Vietnamese girl were working alone at the other.

Kristy's father wanted her to be more like Elizabeth Benton. No, thank you! Anyway, Kristy was a Christian girl. Her father ought to be happy. She wasn't taking dope. She just didn't let musty old rules get in the way of her happiness. After all, "Where the Spirit of the Lord is, there is liberty." That was the motto verse for her youth group, and she liked it.

Kristy glanced at Elizabeth Benton there at the editor's desk. The girl sat quietly, earnestly doing her work. Oh, Elizabeth Benton was just a bore. Worse than that, Kristy knew that for some unknown reason Elizabeth disapproved of her. How could that be? Kristy Peterson was one of the nicest girls in the school. ■

Modesty and Controlled Living

Modesty also indicates emotions that are under control. There is an emotional immodesty which indulges itself in extravagant displays of emotion. To the emotionally immodest, their every tragedy is the worst thing that has ever happened to anybody. Where a balanced person may be mildly happy, the immodest are careening off the walls. Emotions need expression, but the acceptance of limits is the key to balance.

Modesty also indicates emotions that are under control.

There are certain limits outside of which the expression of emotions are improper and even dangerous. Modesty has no inordinate need for attention, because of a calm self-acceptance and self-possession.

Modern American athletics, for example, has made a hero out of the bragging, extravagant, arrogant athlete. In victory he is excruciatingly boring. In defeat he is sullen and graceless.

With an effortless, poetic style that belied his slashing power, B.B. Wilson sliced through a gap in the line and broke into the secondary. In three steps from a three-point stance, the brilliant back would be at a dead run. No other tailback in the NFL had his combination of blinding speed, quick moves and strength.

Wilson saw the rookie cornerback coming and reacted with an instinctive move that cannot be taught. He slowed his speed imperceptibly, causing the overzealous young defender to get to the intersection just a fraction of a second too soon. Wilson gave a head fake right, "juked" left and shot past the confused kid with one of his patented bursts of speed.

The tailback glided untouched into the end zone. The dejected cornerback followed him, unable even to make it look close. Wilson slammed the ball into the turf, somersaulted backward landing on his feet and boogied comically, his legs wobbling like a seasick sailor's. The home crowd loved it! The cheers fell about him like latter-day rain.

A second later he was caught up in a wave of exuberance as his teammates joined him in their customary end-zone celebration for which they were becoming famous. He lifted both index fingers above his head and, puncturing the air in a staccato rhythm, began leading the exultant crowd in their favorite chant.

"Num-ber one! Num-ber one! Num-ber one!"

Turning toward the bench, he began to jog briskly across the field, punctuating each step by jabbing a finger skyward. "Num-ber one! Num-ber one!" Wilson fell, almost drunken with the triumphant mantra.

At the hash mark on the far side he came face-to-face with the crestfallen cornerback who had yielded the end zone without a squabble. They faced each other for a second there in open field before fifty-five thousand screaming fans.

Face-to-face with the rookie, Wilson suddenly, spontaneously bent his knees slightly and, in full view of the spellbound stadium, with his lower body made an obscene gesture at the cornerback.

"You're mine, sweetheart!" Wilson taunted the boy.

In a split second the rookie was on him in a fury. Both benches emptied, and the stands went wild. The fight was fairly brief, and no one was really hurt. Later five or six players, including Wilson and the rookie, were fined. One local newscaster complained about Wilson's "bad taste," and there were words of protest from the visiting coach. But the next Friday night on local high school football fields in thousands of American towns, the lurid gesture was mimicked to the spontaneous laughter and the pretended shock of the local fans. ◼

Modesty proclaims that it is not necessary for a thirteen-year-old boy to enter a room like an entire roller derby team. That is just not necessary. It is neither proper nor modest. Boys must be taught that doors need not be kicked open. And yet, on the other hand, we dare not squelch their childlike enthusiasm for life. Modesty is not passionless living. It is passion under control; it is passion which accepts the limits of propriety.

We usually think of modesty mainly in connection with clothing and fashion. It is uselessly legalistic to ask such questions as how short is too short and how sheer is too sheer. The more important questions about modest dress have to do with being showy or inappropriately seeking attention. Immodesty may have as much to do with excessiveness as with brazenness. In that sense, then, one might have an immodest hairstyle that is excessive and flamboyant and demands attention.

Modesty that is fastidious and judgmental will become legalistic to say the least. It is false modesty that nitpicks and criticizes youthful enthusiasm and discourages joy and vitality.

Such pharisaism binds people up and is hateful.

Guidelines to Modesty

The Christian asks what styles of dress, make-up and hair are acceptable. Listing is petty, soon dated and may miss the point entirely. Yet some guidelines to modesty may be helpful.

- Always be suspicious of the flamboyant. Remember you are trying to express the orderly, decent, modest glory of God through the way you dress.
- Instantly suspect fads.
- In clothing, particularly, try to avoid those styles that are provocative and draw attention to your body.

Now again I want to state that there is a balance here. Holiness does not always have to look like it has been thrown away. We have been through that in generations past.

An inner conviction to seek modesty requires Christians to look in the mirror and honestly ask themselves some searching questions. Are these clothes just slightly too tight? Is this dress just a little too low-cut? Will these clothes be an unnecessary temptation to others?

You do not want to be the center of attention. You want Jesus to be the center of attention.

Modesty is the quiet, dignified celebration of the sacredness of one's privacy with God. Recently a young actress explained her nudity in a movie by asking, "Well, what about Adam and Eve? They were naked in the Garden of Eden. I'm not ashamed of my body either."

What about Adam and Eve? In the first place, they did not even know they were naked. What a wonderful naiveté that must have been. If you can return to that, then you only have to deal with one other fact: There are five and a half billion other people who certainly know when someone is unclothed. Further, that which is used for a shameful purpose becomes shameful. And that which is used to incite lust or cause guilt in others is shameful. But your body is not shameful.

Of her short skirt, a woman said, "Well, my legs are my best feature, and I'm going to show them off." Without realizing it, she is asking for the rejection of herself as a person. She will never feel good about herself if she believes that her legs are her best feature.

God is for the body. Your body is holy, a living sacrifice, acceptable unto God. You do not want to inspire the unhealthy attention of others. You do not want to be the center of attention. You want Jesus to be the center of attention.

It is perfectly reasonable for a Christian woman to look in a mirror and ask herself, Could I do with less makeup? No woman is going to go to hell because of makeup. I am not saying that too much makeup is the Big Sin. But a modest woman learns to ask herself, Can I use makeup within the limits of propriety? Does a woman have to put her eye makeup on till it reaches all the way to her ears?

The modest man learns to look in the mirror and ask himself some questions as well. Do I feel comfortable with myself and is God glorified when my shirt is unbuttoned three buttons down to display a perfectly tanned chest? A Christian man need not ooze worldliness. Let him search his heart first, then his wardrobe and jewelry.

It is *not* legalistic and pharisaical for a teenage boy to look at himself in the mirror and say, Now that I'm saved and filled with the Holy Spirit, I want to serve God. I have always worn my blue jeans so tight they looked as if they were spray-painted on. But do I have to go on wearing them like that?

It is *not* too much to expect that he reinspect his entire wardrobe and hairstyle in search of a more modest, restrained, controlled way of living.

It would be easy if the "Ninety-seven Rules From God About Modesty" were to descend from heaven. Thou shalt not wear heels over a quarter-inch. That is what the Pharisees thought they had. They were wrong. They became legalistic and hateful. Their modesty was as fleshly as the prostitute's immodesty. There are no rules like that. God will not give us those. Instead, we must make decisions about makeup, clothing, attire and all related matters because our hearts are His home and our bodies are a living sacrifice to Him.

Heavenly Father, overrule our rebellious hearts. Lord, so fasten our eyes on Jesus that the way we dress may be an expression of the living, holy, acceptable sacrifices we are. We do not want sin in our own lives. We do not want to cause sin in the lives and eyes of others. God, we do not want the world to think Christians are out-of-control children. We want to be restrained, mature and balanced, manifesting the fruit of the Spirit which is self-control. We want to honor the limits of propriety joyfully. Nay, Lord, more than to accept them, help us to celebrate the fact that lines and limitations are what give life dignity and worthiness. And, Lord, how wonderful to know that we do not have to set laws for ourselves or for each other. Thank You that, if we will be sensitive and yielded and obedient, You will teach us what is proper and wholesome and good. Amen.

VI

FRUGALITY

The Framework of Prosperity

When a society loses frugality from among its moral hardware, the corporate soul begins to twist like sheet metal in a blast furnace. Frugality is that virtue whose absence hits at the very substance of life — poverty of every kind will follow. But it will be even worse than that. Such a society without frugality loses its capacity to evaluate what is really precious.

If the base, the precious and the semi-precious all look alike to a society, it becomes unable to discern the difference between humanity and plastic — between life and a bauble. A society is defined in a great part by what it wastes as well as by what it wants.

The toothless hag was terrifying to look at. Duan-pit stared at the fearsome old woman and felt hot tears flood her eyes. The tears began to trace wet streaks down her smooth eleven-year-old cheeks. They dripped without being touched onto her bright native shirt. The chubby-faced little girl made no effort to hide or stem her tears. She did not even lift her little brown hands and wipe them away.

What passes for frugality is often an obsession with smallness and pettiness.

Her mother tried to comfort her. But what comfort could she give? Duan-pit knew that the wretched-looking old creature was buying her from her father. The old procurer carefully counted baht into her father's eager palm. It was a great deal of money for a man as poor as her father.

Duan-pit did not know what would happen to her in Bangkok. Other girls from her mountain tribe had been sold into the whorehouses. She knew that. She had heard the adults talk about it. What she did not know was exactly what a whorehouse was.

She was terrified and confused and hopeless. Sobs began to rack her body like the uncontrollable shakes of malaria. The old woman triumphantly laid the last baht into her father's outstretched hand. That hand quickly closed around the wrinkled, colored money with a finality that made Duan-pit scream.

A few minutes later the man watched as the woman walked briskly away down the winding jungle trail. At the end of a rope, following her like a little lamb, walked his youngest daughter. Her tiny hands were bound behind her back. The old woman totally ignored the child's pitiable howls.

Now, the man said to himself, he could finally get that new radio he had wanted so badly for so long. In fact, the stupid old witch had finally paid so much he could get a case of beer and some cigarettes and a lantern as well as the radio.

He watched the girl a while longer, then turned back toward his hut. He fingered the roll of bills in the pocket of his shorts. Of course, he hated to see the girl go. But what is a girl compared to a radio? ■

Frugality is difficult to teach today because the very word has utterly disappeared from the functional vocabulary of most people. Among those in whose vocabulary it does remain, there is a great deal of confusion about what it really means.

Many identify frugality as mere thriftiness. But the man who is thrifty can easily become stingy, which can then rapidly become loveless, judgmental and withholding.

Stinginess separates us from those who look to us for providential care. Sometimes, wise parents learn, it is better to buy the double-dip ice cream cone, even though you know the child will never finish both dips. Fiscal responsibility dictates that the second dip is a waste of money. But sometimes love must be the law.

Frugality springs from a balanced view of things and life. Stinginess may actually be a lack of frugality. What passes for frugality is often an obsession with smallness and pettiness.

I had a friend in college whose name was Dennis. Dennis prided himself on being frugal. Actually he was dangerously obsessed with money. I remember the great issue of shoelaces in our sophomore year. Before it was over, I was quite sick of Dennis and his shoelaces. He broke a shoelace, and it became a federal case. He complained for two weeks. It was not so much because the shoelace had broken, since he had worn it for years and thought it was about time for it to break. But he complained bitterly that he could only find shoelaces for sale in pairs. How he moaned, "I don't need two. I only need one." He resented the entire American industrial system for only selling shoelaces in pairs.

That is not frugality, and it is not a virtue. It is an obsession with pettiness. God hates petty living.

I heard about a certain Scotsman traveling on an English train. When the conductor came to collect his ticket, the Scotsman complained about the fare. "I refuse to pay it. It costs too much."

The exasperated conductor asked, "What do you mean, it costs too much? That's the announced price. If you don't buy a ticket, you'll be put off."

"I want you to cut the cost in half," whined the Scot.

They argued until the frustrated English conductor finally shouted, "I'll just fix you." Just as the train went over a high trestle above a river, the English conductor threw the Scotsman's suitcase out the window.

The Scotsman screamed, "What's the matter with you, man? You not only want to steal my money. Now you've drowned my only son!"

In such false frugality, we may actually think we are acting virtuously by doing things that are irrational and unethical. Penny-wise and dollar-poor can become a way of life that destroys homes, relationships and businesses.

Stinginess can also cause us to become judgmental toward what we perceive to be the excesses of others. While we ourselves attempt a frugal life-style, the law of

love must preside over our attitudes toward the possessions of others. In other words, God may give another
liberty at one level regarding possessions that He does
not give me. I have neither the right nor the discernment
to decide what God is saying to another. Legalistic judg-
ments about others will make me presumptuous and
condescending. Law separates people. This is not about
imposing a law of frugality on each other. This is about
trying to hear from God about how we can live so as to
cultivate a life-style that is pleasing in His sight and
effective in our pursuit of holiness.

True Frugality

To speak of being frugal implies far more than saving
money. Frugality is not the opposite of generosity. Frugality is rather the opposite of reckless wastefulness.
Frugality, like modesty, has to do with controlled living.
The great point of frugality concerns the purpose of
things.

Frugality is not so much a question of how many things
I own but of their purpose and place in my life.

For example, there is a purpose for leisure in life.
Recreation is to rebuild, to re-*create*. It has a function in
life. Everyone needs those times to recuperate from dif-
ficulties and strenuous tasks. We need times when we do
something just for the fun of it, just to relax and have a
good time. When frugality is lost, however, recreation
gets out of balance.

A man may actually begin to worship his "time on the
lake." Instead of this being a time of recreating and
rebuilding him to be the man of God he ought to be,
recreation begins to stand between him and God. Instead
of edifying him, his recreation destroys him because it
has lost its purpose in his life. It is not enough anymore

simply to go to the lake. Now he must buy a lot on the lake. Soon it is not enough just to have a lot. At first it is. But then he realizes he must also have a dock. Well, my goodness, a man with a dock and no boat is an idiot. Ultimately the boat is not enough. He must have a boat-house. A boathouse and a dock and a boat seem to demand that there be a house as well. So he builds a summer house, which is better than the one he lives in year-round. Now in order to justify the amount of money he has poured into the house at the lake, he must spend more and more time there.

One day he looks at the boat and reasons, Look at this big, beautiful boat and this dinky little motor! I must have been a fool to buy this little motor for such a big boat. I must have a bigger motor. So he buys a 150-horsepower motor. Now he is satisfied with that for a while until he realizes that when he cranks it up, the boat stands straight up in the water. The marvelous new motor *demands* a bigger boat. Consumption without frugality produces an escalating cycle of things without purpose, and thus the power of mammon eats into our life-style.

Now consider the matter of sex. Sex in married life can mean communion. It can mean joy. It can mean intimacy. It is for tender affection and for procreation of the race. And can we just say that, for sheer fun between two married people, sex is hard to beat. Those are proper purposes for sex in marriage. But sex should never be used as an opportunity to prove sexual prowess. It is not for a demonstration of power, for punishment or for the satiation of lust.

Food is for nourishment and strength. It is even for communion and fellowship. But it is never for Epicurean sensuality. There is one kind of gluttony that merely wants great quantities of food. That is a very forthright form of gluttony. But there's another subtler form of gluttony. That form is not so much concerned with the amount of food. Such gluttony demands some perfectly prepared morsel, some delicacy served with just exactly the right kind of beverage on exactly the right kind of china — in the perfect restaurant. Barring that, such gluttony would rather starve.

This way of thinking says that food is not really to satisfy a need for nutriment. It is rather to quench a thirst for an elitist reassurance that I am worthy of the best.

That is, you see, a kind of topside-down gluttony. Hence, it has the purpose of food all out of balance. If we eat ten times what we need, we are gluttons without frugality. If we get to the place where we would rather not eat than to eat in a place that is beneath us, then we are gluttons as well.

The automobile is for travel. A house and furniture are for protection from the elements and for comfort. Apparel is for covering. None of these things should ever be for status or to prove who we are.

In one church I pastored, there was a well-to-do couple. The Sunday they left for a trip to the South, we said good-bye to them after the morning church service. That night they were back in the evening service.

"Did you change your mind?" I asked.

"Well, the air-conditioning was broken on the car, and we couldn't stand it with the windows rolled up," they answered.

"Well, why didn't you just drive with the windows down and have the air-conditioner repaired after you arrived?" I asked in hopeless naiveté.

"Are you joking?" the lady asked in a shocked tone. "Drive with the windows down? People might think we couldn't afford air-conditioning."

They actually delayed their vacation rather than ride with their windows down because they were afraid people would think they could not afford air-conditioning.

Now neither air-conditioning nor the lack of it means anything about frugality. Frugality concerns not the thing itself but what it means in my life.

I remember a certain chap I ran into on an airplane coming out of Los Angeles. As he flopped into the seat beside me, it was obvious he was terribly irritated. Before I could even introduce myself, he announced, "The first thing I want you to know is I never ride coach. My travel agent took care of this. They're always supposed to book me in first class. I admit I didn't check my ticket, but I got here, and the first-class section was full. They've stuck me in coach! I just want you to know I don't travel coach."

I thought he was going to get up and make a public disclaimer to the whole plane. I just could not help myself. I don't know whether or not it was a sin, but I laughed until tears came into my eyes. I tried to explain myself. I even tried to apologize, but the pompous windbag was so ludicrous to me that I could not restrain myself.

Christians often struggle with the wrong question. They ask, Is the added comfort worth the added cost of first class? But that misses the point. It may be more frugal to travel first-class under certain circumstances. The issue is not money but attitude. It is useless to debate whether or not traveling first-class is a sin because it costs more. If I cannot afford to travel coach because I am afraid that people will think I am the kind of bloke who cannot afford first-class, then first class is for me a sin. It is a sin, and only by deliberately, intentionally depriving myself of it will I ever master it.

Frugality and Money

Richard Foster says, "Money is not something that is

morally neutral, a resource to be used in good or bad ways, depending solely upon our attitude toward it."[1]

This is a bit too mystical and brooding for me, but his warning must be heeded. A rather more balanced view is that of John Wesley, who said, "Money is an excellent gift of God if it is used excellently, answering the noblest needs of humanity."[2] To Wesley, you see, money was not the enemy. The enemy is my own sinful nature. Therefore, in order to arrive at a balanced view of money, I must ask myself frugality's simple questions.

Frugality concerns not the thing itself but what it means in my life.

One, what is money for?

Money is for exchange. Money is for activities and purchases which may without corrupting my spirit add education, comfort and beauty to my life and the lives of those I love. Furthermore, money is for the good of humanity and the expansion of the kingdom. Money is never to be used for the purchase of status. Neither is it to be used for the demonstration of power.

Richard Foster used an excellent example of how the misuse of wealth corrupts. In a brilliant parable out of his own childhood, Foster reports that he was a champion marble-shooter. They played for keeps, and he was the best in the whole neighborhood. Finally none of the kids had any marbles left. Richard Foster had them all.

In order to display his wealth and power, he took everyone out to the pond and meticulously threw in his accumulated fortune of marbles. It was a cruel, ruthless and vicious demonstration of power that comes from wealth.[3]

James, in his epistle, talks about the way we treat the

wealthy in church (see James 2:1-9). Often money speaks in church. And it does not always say, "Praise the Lord." Wealthier men frequently have more to say about the spiritual conduct of the ministry. God forbid. This cannot be. If I need advice on the business aspect of the church, I surely want to find that advice and counsel from those who seem to know something about it. I am far more likely to take advice about business from those who have succeeded than from those who have not. But when it comes to the spiritual dynamic of the church, we dare not be cowed by those who hold the purse strings.

Two, who's in charge here?

Am I controlling money, or is it controlling me? When ethical decisions are based on the bottom line of finances, money is in control. Take, for example, the preachers who fall into sin and need to take time away from their ministries to reconcile with God. Those pastors may reason that their ministries will suffer irreparable damage financially if they are absent for a time. They may be tempted to carry on with the ministry even though their spirits need restoration.

Now the issue has transcended the original sin that clouded their ministries. It has become an issue of exactly who is Lord here. Are we making our decisions according to God or mammon? Man cannot serve two masters at one time. he will always love one and hate the other. Pastors, like all other people, cannot serve God and money (Matt. 6:24). Frugality does not justify spiritual compromise.

By making a decision based on financial need, he has proven that he is not frugal. Money has lost its purpose. Instead of providing for his ministry, money now directs the work. In fact, it controls his life. He has forgotten what he once knew. Expediency corrupts faith like demonic rust. The issue is not money. The real issues are authority, submission, humility, obedience, holiness, patience and faith. These far outweigh the immediate financial needs of his ministry. If the entire ministry sinks, so be it. God can raise it up again. Or maybe it does not need to be raised up again.

Money must never control us. We must control it. I do not believe there is some mystical, evil power inherent in the dollar bill. What I do believe is that there is a weakness in my own flesh. Therefore I must humble myself under the hand of God. I must show mammon who is in charge here: It is the Lord Jesus Christ and not mammon.

Three, will I let virtue set the limits?

Am I willing for God to limit aspects of my life through a commitment to frugal living? In other words, when there is not sufficient money for me to pursue a certain course of action, am I willing to believe that it is not God's will for me to do it now? We easily confess that the positive abundance of funds can be used by God to affirm a course of action. But if that is true, the contrary must also be true. From time to time God may pull tight the purse strings in order to stop me from a course that is not in His will. Therefore lack of funds may be a way that God can use my conviction for frugal, modest living to keep me from continuing in a path that is wrong for me.

Frugality is the willingness to endure limits on myself. This is the problem with the American credit system. Credit allows me to consume at a level of superficial prosperity which is not based on any real wealth. Sooner or later, of course, the piper must be paid. Bankruptcy in

> *When ethical decisions are based on the bottom line of finances, money is in control.*

America comes dressed in a tuxedo, not in rags. Fooled by their own mirage of wealth, Americans are amazed when financial disaster hits them.

I find it difficult to discover a vocabulary rich enough to express this to modern Westerners. It is possible to do without some things. My wife, Alison, and I once shared a weekend retreat with some young couples. We told them how we got married when we were nineteen and seventeen years old. I asked, "Do you realize we were married four years before we ever bought a car?"

My wife and I were shocked at the communication gap which instantly cracked open and widened before our eyes. They could not get it. They could not understand the words.

They said, "What do you mean, you didn't have a car?"

I said, "I'm trying to tell you. We didn't own an automobile."

They gaped like modern children quizzically inspecting some ancient agricultural implement.

"We just don't know what you're talking about. How did you get around?"

I said, "I walked. I hitchhiked to school. I hitchhiked home. I hitchhiked to my first job. At midnight when that one was over, I hitchhiked to my second job. I rode the bus."

"Rode the bus?" they marveled.

Provoked by their astonishment, I plunged on. "Do you realize," I said, "that we were married for three years before we ever owned a couch? We had an old army cot on which my wife arranged folded quilts so it looked flat. She made a little coverlet that lay across it and hung to the floor. It looked just like a couch. But it was an army cot. If anybody came to visit, we would caution them, 'No, don't sit on the couch.' But if they came in too fast and sat on it, the pitiful contraption would shoot out from the wall, hurling their legs in the air like a carnival ride."

The young couples could not get enough of this rime of an ancient mariner.

"We couldn't afford it," I said, knowing the phrase would be quaint if not meaningless to them.

"What do you mean, you couldn't afford it?" they asked. "Why didn't you just charge it?"

I realized then that we were speaking completely different languages.

We must again master the primeval art of waiting on things until we can pay for them. I hate to see the use of money disappear from the American culture. Plastic cards destroy virtue. Because it creates a mirage of prosperity, credit becomes a self-made Sword of Damocles. Cars, houses, furniture and clothing are hung there even as it dangles above my own head. Sooner or later the whole thing will fall on me if I have no real wealth. Plastic kills!

A Further Question for the Virtuous

Sooner or later frugality asks an even deeper question. Not only am I willing to live as I can afford to, but am I willing to live on less than I can afford? Can I do without this? For the sake of the self-discipline or simply because it is not a wise expenditure, there are times to forego even that which I *can* afford.

It is a sinful arrogance indeed to assume that since I have ten million dollars, I can afford to use even one to light cigars. I can *never* afford to do that. The exercise of that kind of carnal abuse of finances will destroy a soul. At that point we are misusing money to demonstrate power and express affluence. That gives no glory to God. It helps nobody. It is wrong to burn money on the end of a cigar when there are people who are starving to death.

Frugality and Repentance

To see financial restitution as a proper use of money is unfamiliar to modern Westerners, especially Protestants. But it was not to the ancient Jew.

If I live a frugal life with a balanced view of money, what about prosperity in my life?

Jesus looked up into the tree and called out to Zacchaeus, "Come down, little fellow. I'm going to have lunch with you."

The man's response was immediate. Zacchaeus said, "I've cheated the poor. I confess."

Just like that! He confessed, "I'm a cheat." But he went on to say, "Here's what I'm going to do, Lord. I'm going to give half of all that I have to the poor. To everyone I've cheated, I will pay them back four times."

Jesus perceived that Zacchaeus's entire attitude toward money had changed. Money no longer had a hold on the little man. The power of mammon was broken, right there on that limb.

Jesus said, "Salvation has come to this house today" (see Luke 19:1-10). The word that Jesus used might well be translated *deliverance*. Jesus announced, "This man has been delivered, and his whole household has been set free from the controlling power of mammon." Zacchaeus proved Jesus right through his new and proper use of money.

In other words, if I have cheated anyone, frugality demands that I pay it back. If I owe anyone money, I will fix my goal on paying the debt. If I have withheld my tithe, I must now give it and more — much more! I must give until I am free.

The Place of Prosperity

If I live a frugal life with a balanced view of money, what about prosperity in my life? I think the church has often failed to communicate a balanced view of prosperity. On the one hand we have the hyper-spiritual who say money is altogether evil. Get it away from you. Give it away. Do not have anything to do with it. It is nasty and dirty and filthy, and it has a spirit in it that will get you. But then along comes a need to pay for something in the church, and we ask folks to give money. You see, having told them how bad it is, we now ask God to give them enough of it to give some to the church.

On the other hand, others say God is a God of riches. God wants to bless you, they reason, and if you are right with God and have a correct confession, you are going to be rich. Now if you are not rich, it must be because you are not right with God. Stranded in between these two extremes is the great body of people who are living day to day on the money which they can earn while trying to provide for their families and improve their lives. What can we say to them? There is nothing inherently evil about needing or having the finances to get by in this life. John Wesley had a magnificent equation for this. He said, Earn all you can. Earn it righteously. Earn it in a way that brings no shame to people and no shame to God. Earn all you can.

Second, save all you can. Now saving all you can does not mean hoarding it. It means setting limits on my life-style in order that more might be made available to the kingdom of God and not go up in the smoke of mere consumerism. Saving all you can is crucial to frugality.

Earn all you can. Save all you can. But then Wesley adds the missing element: Give all you can. Frugality saves to give. Greed gives to get. Frugality plots and plans and schemes and denies self and sacrifices in order to give more next year than I gave this year.

I want to suggest that you have a family meeting. Now ask yourselves, What can we do to give more than we gave last year? Is there any way we can live a more modest life, something we can do without, some excess we can lay aside in order that we may make a better investment in the kingdom of God than we have ever made? I believe that is pleasing to God. It will engage your family's attention for the things of the kingdom and draw their eyes away from the power of mammon.

Earn all you can. Save all you can. ...Give all you can.

Conclusion

Frugality is the flinty virtue which will set me free from the terrible grip of mammon. Without frugality the frayed thread by which civilization hangs above the pit will surely give way. What a sick irony it will be if the extra weight in our own arms — the weight of all we hold valuable — is what finally snaps the thread.

It is sad when violence and rapine sweep the land and we encounter the medieval horror of roving brigands who storm our castles. But whatever will history say of us if we knock over our own walls using golden battering rams and let the ravenous beasts in upon our babies? It may not be immorality that finally snaps the fragile thread of virtue. It may be the price of a pair of designer tennis shoes.

Carlton Butler slowly rocked and stared out the window at the car in his driveway. A hard morning rain was falling, and everyone else was still asleep.

Carlton Butler did not understand his daughter's relationship with Howard Hart. How his daughter could get hooked up with such a person he had no idea. Betty had been raised in the Baptist church. This man had no morals at all. In amassing his huge fortune, he had already destroyed two marriages and made himself a worldwide reputation as a womanizer.

Now they were sleeping together under his roof. He had never thought he would tolerate such a thing. When Betty wrote from New York that Hart was coming home with her for the holidays, Carlton had not expected them to share a room. What would people say?

But Howard Hart *was* famous — a real Hollywood type — and, well, Carlton reckoned those folks just didn't think like Baptists from rural Alabama. One thing was sure. There was no denying the fact that he had given Betty a Maserati. Think of that! Well, let them talk. Let them go choke. They were all just jealous of Betty. They had always been jealous.

She was the prettiest, most talented girl in the state. When she went off to New York for a modeling career, the neighbors talked. When she did a magazine fold-out, they surely talked. When she started dating the famous Howard Hart, they talked. Well, let them talk!

Hart had more than hinted that if he and Betty got married, he would gladly pay off the Butler family farm. For years Carlton Butler had been dangerously leveraged on the farm. He had nearly gone under in '84. The $250,000 he owed would be pocket change to a multimillionaire like Howard Hart.

Butler wished they wouldn't sleep together. Especially not under his roof. But this is a new day, he reminded himself. It's not like it used to be. Carlton Butler rocked in his grandfather's squeaky oak rocker and watched the Alabama rain beating down on his daughter's blue Maserati. ■

VII

HONESTY

The Crucifixion of Instinct

In the early 1970s I ministered occasionally in the federal penitentiary at Atlanta. I have no idea whether I helped anyone on those visits. I know they were a constant source of astonishment and education to me.

One man I met there was named Eugene. He had embezzled hundreds of thousands of dollars from a corporation that sold infant products. Yet he complained bitterly that a country music artist had stolen a song he composed. Eugene made a clear distinction between "straightforward embezzlement" and a "low-life thief who'd steal a man's song."

His protestations were not of innocence but of honesty. He never claimed to be innocent. He claimed to be honest about being dishonest. "I'm a thief," Eugene would say, "but at least I'm honest about it."

The really sobering thought, of course, is to consider the country music singer. How did he justify it to himself? I'm no thief! he surely tells himself. I really have no idea where the original idea for that song came from. At least, he probably tells himself, *I* never embezzled anything! Perhaps he even lost the name and address of the convict who mailed him the song.

Honesty is the virtue of wealth and words. Honesty in communication is telling the truth. (Thou shalt not bear false witness.) Honesty in possessions is right action with regard to things. (Thou shalt not steal.)

That is simple enough. The problem is that we are now facing a generation that morally does not know its left hand from its right. The simple biblical injunction of the Law of Moses is quaint if not utterly insensible to the modern Western urbanite.

Honesty and Possessions

Hardly anyone argues philosophically for theft. Even the thief objects when another thief steals his loot. However, the problem is to see honesty's subtle application to our lives. Many modern Americans see theft as armed robbery. Anything short of that, they reason, is actually something else. Casual theft is a major financial and moral problem for America. The teenager who shoplifts, the thrill theft, the unpaid debt; these are the everyday thefts of America. If an individual unnecessarily and deliberately files bankruptcy for the express purpose of avoiding the payment of debt, he is a thief. He has stolen money. To delay repaying a debt until the creditor, in frustration, simply writes it off is thievery. If a housewife arrives at her car and realizes there is one article in her shopping bag which was not actually rung up, and she does not return to pay for it, she is a thief.

Faceless theft has become a justifiable crime. No one excuses robbing an old lady of her Social Security check. But to steal from an institution has become almost heroic. It is different to steal from a company or a corporation, many people think.

Casual theft is a major financial and moral problem for America.

In Warren Beatty's movie about Clyde Barrow, there is a fascinating bank robbery scene. There was an innocent bystander at the counter with his hands up as Bonnie and Clyde robbed the teller. A stack of loose cash was lying on the counter. Finally Clyde Barrow turned his gun on the man and asked, "Whose money is this on the counter?"

The man answered, "It's my money. I haven't made my deposit yet."

"Pick it up," Clyde said, "and put it in your pocket. I don't rob individuals. I only rob banks."

His was a specious logic. Yet, tragically, Clyde may have spoken for untold thousands of Americans who find it perfectly acceptable to defraud an insurance company. After all, we say to ourselves, insurance is a racket itself.

Faceless theft starts with the wrong person. The question is not who or what owns a thing. The point concerns who does not. Respect for private ownership transcends my ability to identify the owner. The fact that it is not mine is the bottom line. It is irrelevant that I do not know the owner.

The moment Susan saw the ring, she knew it was

expensive. She had never seen any real jewelry. The tawdry costume junk that always lay on her mother's dresser was symbolic of the house they lived in and of her whole life. Her world was filled with the cheap and imitation.

Susan furtively looked around the gym. She was alone. The sun through the windows defined bright squares on the dusty expanse of the basketball court. She stepped into one of these golden pools and slowly opened her hand. The ring floated on her palm like some divine artifact fallen to the earth.

It was a diamond! The stone looked like a large one to her. It was surrounded by a sparkling galaxy of green gems all set in brilliant gold. She slid it slowly onto her finger and rotated her hand palm downward until the sun darted through the diamond's prisms with arrogant brilliance. Susan gasped. Surely she had never seen anything so beautiful in her life.

The best part, of course, was that it was now hers. The good fortune of the thing made her feel like giggling. She wondered how many people had walked right past it. She, only she, had seen it half-hidden in the dust near the bleachers. Oh, the tortuous moments waiting for the gym to clear. She had thought the last of the lingering NBA "wannabe's" would never leave. The moment the door closed behind the last boy, Susan had darted to the ring like a hound to the chase. She remembered her exquisite delight when she retrieved the treasure from the dust and perceived its value.

Now she relished the delectable new sensation of luxury. As she studied the brilliant, almost weightless little fleck of light, it seemed to her that a certain magic entered her soul. Suddenly she knew. She was born for rings like this. It looked perfectly natural on her finger. Why, it even fit! She determined, standing there in that warm lake of sunshine, that she would always have things like this, no matter what she had to do.

Suddenly the strangest thought flitted across her brain. I wonder whose ring it is? She giggled at the absurdity of it. The notes of her laughter, like crystal butterflies, danced in the air of the dingy arena. Why, the ring was hers, of course. What a funny thought. What an absolutely funny thing. ■

Prevailing "wisdom" claims that what I do *not* know is crucial to honesty. If I do not know whose thing it is, it may as well be mine. We must rearrange our thinking. Honesty must be based on what I do know. I may not know whose it is, but I certainly know whose it is not. Knowing it is not mine is the true ground of honesty.

The point is not really that I have no right to what is yours. The point is, I have no right to that which is not mine.

Honest Gain

Honest financial advancement is not a dishonorable goal. The selling of worthy goods or services for a fair price is pleasing in God's sight. There is nothing wrong with making a profit and gaining wealth. God wants to prosper His people.

However, the selling of goods for more than they are worth, even though the traffic will bear it, is dishonest. Willfully hiding pertinent information from another in order to get the better of him in a business deal is not shrewd business — it is thievery.

Boynton's Mercedes turned off the main road. The gravel crunched under its wheels like tiny bones in the massive jaws of a great wolf. It was a good, powerful, masculine sound, and he liked it.

A bunny darted across the lane, and he could not resist the impulse to swerve the huge car. He did not hit the cottontail. He did not mean to. But its frightened, erratic journey into the undergrowth made him chuckle. That's one little rabbit with a harrowing tale of near death to share when it gets home.

As he drove, he enjoyed the idyllic scene spread out before him. The leaves on the massive oaks were in full fall plumage. The old gray fence posts and rusted barbed wire traced antique designs across the brown, overgrown fields. Only a few years before, these fields would have been full of cattle. In fact, it was hard to believe he was only an hour and a half from downtown. Right here on this lonely gravel road he felt years away from the madding cross-town connector and his own high-rise office building.

The absence of cattle in the fields was really why he was here. Old lady Weakun was not really farming any of this anymore. And she had no family to help. Mrs. Weakun lived all alone out here.

Why, he was doing her a favor. With the money from this sale, she would be able to live comfortably until she died. Getting away from this farm was what she needed. She was lucky he came along. Anyone else might have really robbed her.

The car phone rang just as the roof and twin chimneys of the Weakun farmhouse nudged into view. As he answered, he noted the sagging roof line jutting above the soft, grassy-brown horizon.

"Hello," he answered.

"Hey, Boynton, it's Carl," the smooth voice of his partner responded. "Are you nearly there?"

"Yes," Boynton answered. "I can see the house from here. Your timing is perfect. What have you got for me?

Is our information correct?"

"I checked with Commissioner Threllkell. It looks like the new loop is going right through the old Weakun place. Have you got the check and the contract? Is she going to sign?"

"Calm down," Boynton reassured him. "It's in the bag. Are you sure your information is good?"

"I told you," Carl purred. "I talked to Threllkell himself. Of course, he wouldn't officially confirm the route."

"Of course." They both chuckled amiably at the Threllkell joke. Threllkell was a fool, and they both knew it. Two weeks in the Bahamas every year assured Threllkell's unofficial dependability. "See you at the office in a few hours. Gotta go."

"Listen, Boynton, do you think the old lady has heard about the new loop yet?" Carl asked. The directness of the question irritated Boynton. Carl's lack of tact was a constant bother to Boynton.

"Don't be silly," he barked and hung up.

Boynton eased the metallic blue Mercedes to a halt in front of the picturesque old house with its wide-sweeping veranda. It would be a real shame to knock this thing over, he thought. A real shame. He stepped out of the Mercedes, stretched his arms over his head and circled the car.

His sure, unhurried steps were those of a wolf circling a crippled doe. Her hind legs broken, there was no need for haste. She was a sure thing now. ■

There is a line between shrewd business and thievery. However, it is not nearly so fine as we are led to believe. We would do far better to bend over backward for honesty. It is better to miss out on the deal than to make it by the slightest deception. It is better to make a minor profit with honesty than a major one without it.

Of course, honesty in selling is no less important than

honesty in buying. Selling something for more than it is worth is dishonest, not clever. The used car lot that sells an automobile knowing that the transmission is on its last leg is operated by a band of thieves. The fact that they used no gun is irrelevant — they are still brigands.

Honest Gain; Honest Got

Gambling has become a controversial issue in the modern church. This is a remarkable turn of events. Historically the church has emphatically opposed gambling. There is no specific Bible verse which says, "Thou shalt not gamble." But the counsel of God taken as a whole clearly teaches that I have no right to another's goods without offering something of value in return. Gambling not only endangers the resources of God entrusted into my hands, but I exploit the passion and lust for chance in the life of another in order to take his goods with nothing in return. When a state or a nation begins to operate gambling games, it breeds characterlessness and immorality into the lives of its citizenry.

It is better to make a minor profit with honesty than a major one without it.

A bingo game for money in the church hall is no cute diversion for elderly Christians. It is gambling. It is the church playing Russian roulette with its own soul.

The great need in America now is for moral leadership. The end *never* justifies the means. Do not be fooled by how many textbooks a state lottery will buy. Consider the single mother in the ghetto who will bet her children's lunch money on a three-digit number. Forget the building project financed with bingo. Remember the ten-year-old who cannot make the distinction between his grand-mother's beloved priest and his father's hated bookie.

We dare not make decisions based on expediency. We dare not allow the state to steal the money of the poor or the church to pander to our lust for chance.

The exaggerated advertisement and the padded expense account have almost become fixtures of American business. Deliberately shaved tax forms are submitted without hesitation, not by Mafia chieftains but by middle-class churchgoers. Employees chronically arrive late and leave early, never even considering their theft of time and salary. And employee theft of tools and goods now reaches into the billions annually.

Possessions are significant because they come from God. They are entrusted into our stewardship. How we handle possessions, our own and those of others, is important. It is important because it is important to God.

Honesty in Communication

Honesty is correct relationship with the highest level of reality. God Himself is ultimate reality. Therefore truth is sacred. Departure from truth is departure from God. Therefore the issue of truth is crucial to what we believe to be true about God and life.

Satan is a liar and the father of lies. Therefore those who operate in right relationship to ultimate truth live in right relationship to who God is. They reflect the character of their Father. Those who deal in deception reveal who their true father is. Satan is the father of and the center of all deception in the earth.

True Truth and False Truth

There may be things that are true, but they are not the

truth. Abraham and Sarah went to Egypt. Abraham knew the Egyptians would see that Sarah was beautiful. They might well desire to have her. Abraham also knew that he was defenseless. If they wanted his wife, they might kill him to take her. Therefore he said, "She is my sister." It was true. Sarah was his half-sister. They shared the same father by different mothers. She was his sister. The higher reality, of course, was that she was his wife. It was true, but it was not the truth.

True statements can even be woven together to form an untruth. The classic example is the first mate who wrote in the log book, "Captain was sober today." The captain may have been sober every day. But the implication was that the captain's sobriety was a happy and rare occurrence. The very way the mate included that statement, a true statement, created an untruth. A true statement can be made an untruth.

The first mate, in deception, manipulation and innuendo, brings disharmony into the ship. The second mate sees the spurious entry and asks, "Does the captain have a problem with alcohol?" The first mate says nothing. He only shrugs his shoulders and rolls his eyes. He has silently lied yet again.

Now the first mate goes to the captain and says, "Captain, you just might like to know that the second mate asked me today if you have a chronic problem with alcohol." Again, it was a true statement. Yet it became a sordid, manipulative lie by painting an untrue picture.

In this way the difference is clear between a true statement and the truth. There is also a contrast between an untruth and a lie. The matter of a lie has to do with motive. A father says to his child, "Tomorrow we'll go to the park." But a great earthquake bursts the nation open from sea to sea, and the city park slides into oblivion. The six-year-old does not care about the earthquake. He announces, "We're going to the park today." The father explains, "No, the park is no more. It's gone." The child pouts, "You lied!" Did the father lie? He certainly did not. Did he tell an untruth? He did.

Maturity understands the delicate balance between an untruth and a lie. On the one hand the issue is guile or motive. The problem on the other hand is cold-blooded literalism.

I was visiting in the parsonage of a fellow pastor. He had a cute little four-year-old son. At one point I tweaked the lad's nose, pushing the end of my thumb through my fingers. "I've got your nose!" I announced triumphantly.

The little boy pleaded jokingly, "No, give me back my nose! Give me back my nose!"

Then in a minute I'd grab it again. "Got your nose, got your nose."

After a few minutes his preacher father said, in front of the child, "I'd thank you not to do that again. I just make it a practice not to lie to my children, and you're not helping me teach that."

I had, in fact, told the child an untruth. I did not get the boy's nose. I state that now in print. I would have *liked* to have gotten his father's nose. That kind of smug literalism draws a tiny little circle of truth and rejects all joy of fantasy or jest.

Every parent must make the determination about how to relate to truth and fantasy. My wife and I never indulged in the Santa Claus myth with our children. We told our children from the beginning that Santa is strictly a cultural legend. There is, of course, no such thing as Santa Claus, but many fine parents do teach their children to believe in him. But we were straightforward with our own children. I felt this determination served our own goals best. I am not attempting to heap condemnation on anyone. Our own reasons were two-fold. One was that we felt it was closely related to the issue of theology. I did not want to have to explain to a wide-eyed eight-year-old that, yes, I know I told her there was a Santa Claus. However, Jesus actually is real. "I've got your nose" seems to fall into quite a different category.

The second reason was more self-serving. I did not encourage the Santa Claus myth because, I reasoned, why should I shell out all that money every year and let some guy who doesn't even exist get all the credit?

Literalism will make our lives joyless and uncreative. Cordell Hull was the secretary of state under Franklin D. Roosevelt. Hull was an infamous literalist. Riding a train across the Midwest, the secretary and some others observed a flock of sheep in a field. Someone said, "I see all these sheep have already been sheared." Cordell Hull protested, "No, I don't think we can safely state that. All we can be sure of is that those sheep have been sheared on the side facing the train."

Having admitted that such priggishness is indeed galling, it is equally certain that it is not the greater issue.

There are two kinds of dishonest communication. The first is simulation; the second is dissimulation.

Simulation is to seem to be what we are not. *Dissimulation* is to seem not to be what we are.

Simulation

Simulation includes all those deceptive practices of image alteration so ingrained in modern society. The craft of simulation includes such tools as exaggeration, pretense and hypocrisy. The image-conscious society in which we live hates the truth and loves the appearance.

An unspoken pact of mutual deception rules the land like a cruel monarch. You pretend to believe my image and I will pretend to accept yours. We both know the other is spinning out simulation like a spider's web. We both know it is not reality, and we both know the other knows it. But we agree to the silent deception because it suits us both.

Religion no less than politics or business plays the simulation game. Sometimes it is no more than mere exaggeration to appear more spiritual or caring or successful or something than we really are. Sometimes it is the crass, Hollywood manipulation of television audiences and Sunday congregations for evil purposes.

Simulation is to seem to be what we are not. Dissimulation is to seem not to be what we are.

I was visiting another parsonage one Sunday afternoon. We all enjoyed a lovely dinner and settled in to watch a football game.

At halftime the pastor got up and left the room for ten minutes or so. Later at the evening service, where I was to preach, the pastor told the congregation, "I just want to tell you that I made a pastoral call this afternoon. I spent some time talking with Sister Wilson. She's much better."

I was frankly amazed to hear this report. After the service I said to the pastor, "You know, we've been friends for a long time. I'm not trying to call your hand. I just want to understand. You said you went to the hospital this afternoon. But we watched football all afternoon. I don't think there's anything wrong with two preachers watching football, but you said you went to the hospital."

He laughed and said, "No, I didn't. I never said I went to the hospital. You weren't listening. Remember when I went out at halftime? I spent ten minutes on the phone with that lady."

"Yes," I replied, "but you gave your people the impression that you went to the hospital."

"What does it hurt if they think their pastor made a visit on Sunday afternoon instead of watching a ball game?" he asked.

The story of Ananias and Sapphira is evidence of God's seriousness about religious simulation (Acts 5:1-11). They were not slain for withholding money. They died for claiming more generosity and gracious faith than they had. That sobering little story is about honesty.

We financially support ministries that are experts in simulation.

The American church has created an atmosphere that is conducive to simulation. We are shocked and repulsed by the bogus evangelist who claims to operate in the word of knowledge while actually receiving radio transmissions from a hidden sound booth. What a reproach! What a horrifying scandal!

The man will certainly answer to God. But the American church is not blameless. We are sending ministries mixed signals. We financially support ministries that are experts in simulation. Then we hate them when they are exposed. We embrace the hyper-spiritual, flamboyant image-makers and their puppet preachers. We demand that they *not* tell us the truth. But we despise their public nakedness.

Could it be that the famous preacher with the private bondage of pornography is imprisoned by his religious public that rejects the internal reality of his humanity while embracing his public success?

Dissimulation

Dissimulation is appearing *not* to be what we really are. This is perhaps the common crisis of faith for the average Western believer.

The soft conversation and rippling good humor among those lounging in the courtyard belied the tragedy being played out inside. But it made it easier for the burly fisherman to rest unnoticed against the wall of the high priest's house. It was crazy for him to be here. If they had arrested Jesus Himself, His followers would be in even greater danger.

But he just couldn't stay away. Confused, disoriented and nearly distraught, he had followed the miserable little band of temple guards from Olivet to the Antonia fortress and on to this foreboding place. He should leave. What could he do to help? Yet something rooted him to the ground.

The evening closed in on Peter like a clammy hand. He shivered and drew his robe tighter. Peter stared at the flickering torch light from within Caiaphas's mansion. The random outbursts and shouting from inside filled him with fear and dread.

The night watchman, several cronies and a couple of bored soldiers stood near a bed of glowing embers. The fire drew Peter like a magnet. Soon his massive hands were warming over the radiant coals.

"Here's one of them," a girl's voice interrupted his mournful thoughts. "That big guy is a follower of Jesus."

Across the fire from him a slender adolescent pointed her delicate finger right between his eyes. His sad concern for his Master drained away. In its place flooded gripping fear. Peter had never felt so naked. Was this the way he would end? Denounced in a shadowy courtyard by a mere servant girl?

The soldiers around him stirred. Their interest mildly awakened, they turned their eyes on the craggy figure who shared their fire. Peter sensed instantly that this could get very dangerous in moments. These wolves awakened could be lethal.

Peter began to curse and swear. "I tell you, I don't know this Jesus. I don't know the man!"

Now, no matter how close to the fire he stood, Peter could not seem to get warm. Surely this courtyard was the coldest place in Israel on this evil night (see Matt. 26:69-75).

Most Christians will never be tempted to deny Christ before a firing squad. Few, relatively speaking, will be tortured to denounce His name. Far more often it is by silence or a head nod or a knowing wink that the modern believer denies his allegiance to Christ.

"I do not know Him" is the subtle dissimulated message of the collaborator. The compromised servant without the courage to speak his conviction denies who he is. The tolerated dirty joke at the water cooler becomes a trap of dissimulation for the cowardly.

Let your "yea be yea and your nay be nay," the Bible says (see Matt. 5:37). That may very well mean saying yes to Jesus when it is costly and no to the world when it is unpopular. The temptation will seldom be to outright denial, but rather to subtle compromises. Soft public dissimulation is the velvet-lined coffin of dynamic faith.

The Instinct for Dishonesty

The motivation for dishonesty is the animal instinct for self-preservation. The flesh says, If I want it, I'll steal it. If I am not, I'll pretend to be. If I am, I'll pretend not to be. If I want to sell it, I will not tell everything. What can possibly shatter the spell of so inborn an instinct?

Proverbs 22:4 says, "By humility and the fear of the Lord are riches, and honour, and life." Babies are not born with the fear of God. They are born with the instincts of wolf cubs. Parents, governments, schools and institutions are to instill the fear of God. If they fail, the child grows more lupine every day.

The motivation for dishonesty is the animal instinct for self-preservation.

The second motivation to crucify the instinct of self-preservation *is* inborn. In every man there is the thumbprint of the Creator. It is a homesickness for the image of God. Once awakened, this longing for a character of godliness is a fierce power. There is great joy in moving from glory to glory.

The closer a man lives to reality and truth, the more fully this inner longing is awakened. "Ye shall know the truth, and the truth shall make you free" (John 8:32) is not mere church rhetoric. It is the mystery key to full humanity in the image of God.

Listen to the howling of the wolves. Cynical Pilate, staring quizzically into the face of the Lamb of God, asked his infamous question: "What is truth?"

Now listen to the voice of God.

I am the way, the truth, and the life (John 14:6).

Wolves have no concern for virtue. They care nothing for truth. Raw meat is enough for them. They never seek to break the horrible bondage of instinct and liberate the spirit. Wolves live by instinct.

By clutching at the instinct to live, men and women die as wolves. By dying to instinct, they become fully alive and truly human. Crucifixion is painful. And no crucifixion is more painful than the denial of an instinct. Yet it is on just that very cross that the poor fallen sons of Adam are lifted up to glory.

VIII

MEEKNESS

The Control of Power

S ammy Eubanks was the guiding light for his own flock of nearly six thousand souls. He was also "Your Television Pastor" to hundreds of thousands "across America and in nineteen wonderful countries," as he was fond of saying. His down-home charm and boyish good looks had taken him a long way from his poverty-stricken childhood in Antlers, Oklahoma.

Eubanks crossed his legs and leaned back in his Brazilian leather office chair. He flicked an imaginary speck of lint from his taupe trousers and hooked his thumbs under his suspenders. This was his own patented pose for which he was famous. His devotees and critics alike mimicked the gesture. He had practiced it in front of a mirror until he had just the right nuances. It said to his largely Southern evangelical audience, "This is a good ol' boy." But the fact that the trousers were hand-tailored in Milan and the suspenders cost nearly $200 was not unnoticed by many of his most prosperous supporters.

Eubanks's slickly packaged message of prosperity and self-image had found a ready market. His last book, *No More an Okie*, had sold nearly 600,000 copies. The ministry's private plane, named "The Wings of Glory," was a state-of-the-art jet that had been donated by a Las Vegas casino owner named Gino Pantolli. Eubanks poo-pooed the hue and cry about the man's Mafia connections. Instead he had read a letter from Pantolli on TV about how the casino boss had used a "partners' prayer cloth" and made three million dollars in a single week.

"The wealth of the sinful is laid up for the righteous!" Eubanks had proclaimed. "If God wants to get a plane to this ministry through Las Vegas — well, hallelujah!"

The phrase brought exultant cheers from his congregation every time he used it.

"Pastor Eubanks," his secretary's voice over the intercom broke into his thoughts.

"Yes, Marlene, what is it?"

"Rev. Flack is here. Shall I show him in?"

"Yes, bring him right in," Eubanks answered brightly.

This was it. He had been waiting for this moment for weeks. Ever since he had first received the pictures, Eubanks had been looking forward to this very moment.

The door opened, and Marlene said, "Here's Rev. Flack, pastor."

"Thank you, Marlene," Sammy said warmly. "Come in, Myron. It's so good to see you!"

The two men shook hands as the door clicked shut discreetly behind them.

"Have a seat, Myron. Have a seat. Let's relax and talk this over. Now come on. I'm sure it's not as bad as it looks," Sammy purred. He studied the older man's face. So this was "the giant" in defeat.

Myron Flack was a real pioneer in televangelism. His ministry went all the way back to the big years of tent crusades. His healing ministry had been at the very top for years. Now at nearly sixty-five, Flack and his ministry had lost some ground to several younger, flashier upstarts like Sammy Eubanks. But he was still a biggie. Myron Flack was an institution more than a ministry. Now he was in the palm of Sammy Eubanks's hand.

"How are you doin', Myron?" Sammy asked as the older man eased into the stuffed chair across from him. "Is Margarita handlin' things all right? Or maybe I should ask what all does she know?"

"Look," Myron Flack said, "let's cut through the baloney. What do you want?"

Sammy was surprised at how weak Flack's voice was. That booming voice that could stand 'em on end in the back row was a gravelly whisper now. Flack looked horrible. He was unnaturally pale. A limp mask of grief made his somewhat doughy features sag. He looked like a lump of clay that might run out on the Oriental carpet at any moment.

"Want?" Sammy asked in mock surprise. "I don't *want* anything except to help."

"They told me you had the pictures," Flack said, dropping his eyes.

"Yes — yes, I do," Eubanks said. With that he pulled them from their brown folder on the desk and fanned them out dramatically. "I have these, anyway. Are there more?"

Flack's pained eyes panned the lurid black and whites.

An involuntary moan escaped his lips. "No, that's — that's all. Put them away — please."

Sammy left the pictures just where they lay.

"Well, this is pretty bad stuff, Myron. Pretty shocking. What can I do to help?"

"Help?" Flack looked up in surprise. "Help? Why, you can show me some mercy, Sammy. You can put those pictures in the fire and let me quietly retire. Can you do that? That's not a lot, is it?"

Meekness is the manliest virtue.

Sammy wanted to vomit. Was this whining, sad old sack of potatoes the lion of God who had taught a whole generation about faith? He was disgusting!

"Why, no, Myron," Sammy said. "That's not too much. I don't intend to do anything. As far as I'm concerned this is the end of it."

"Really, Eubanks?" Flack asked incredulously. "Do you mean it? You have the power to crush the life out of me now."

"Yes," said Sammy, "I suppose I do. But, hey — aren't we brothers in the kingdom?"

"Yes!" agreed Flack. "Yes, of course we are. I just...."

"Now, now. That's the end of it. You just go on home to Margarita and tell her everything's fine."

The two men stood and embraced as brothers indeed. The obvious gratitude in Flack's eyes was a surprise to Eubanks. At the door Flack turned to stare into the younger man's eyes.

"You know," he said. "I have learned something in this. I may have been wrong about pain, Sammy. I may have been wrong about a lot of things."

With that he was gone, and Eubanks returned to his desk. He paused for a second then picked out one particular photo from the scattered pile. He studied it for a moment and whistled softly between his teeth. He seized the phone from the cradle and rang Marlene's desk.

"Marlene, get Harry Grimes at the *News Herald* on the phone for me, will you, please. And call Jim Nance down in the administration office. Tell him I want his best estimate of all Myron Flack's assets on my desk in three hours."

The Rev. Sammy Eubanks leaned back in his chair and closed his eyes. "Praise the Lord," he thought. "This is going to mean some real big openings." He pressed a button on his desk and all the lights in the office dimmed. It lent the office a cave-like atmosphere. ∎

Meekness, the Manly Virtue

Meekness is the manliest virtue. Misunderstood by many, meekness is often thought to be only for the weak-sister types. Nothing could be further from the truth. It is the supreme virtue of leadership. It is the virtue without which power becomes tyranny. Meekness is power under control.

Christianity itself is a paradox that turns topside down the world's comprehension of what it means to live triumphantly. In that sense meekness is the epitomal virtue.

Now in all virtues there is what might be called the conviction of the virtue. That is what we believe to be true about it. Then there is its theater of operation. That is, there is some circumstance necessary to put the virtue in action. Fear, for example, must be present or courage cannot be called into action. Just so, the ascent to power is the universe of meekness.

A big boy hits a small boy. The small boy endures it quietly. He has no other option. Inwardly, however, he seethes with lust for revenge. Because he is subdued in the face of violence, we may mislabel him as meek. Yet he is actually consumed with murderous rage. Perhaps he intellectually forsakes vengeance, but he is not meek. He is simply resigned.

However, suppose it is the small boy who hits the larger fellow. The offended boy has the power to break the little guy in half. Yet he bears it quietly. That's meekness.

There are two words which together paint a completely wrong picture of meekness. Those two words are *meek* and *little*. We often say, "He is a meek little fellow." Immediately a sort of Casper Milquetoast image is conjured up. We envision this man as an ineffectual, impotent, weak, powerless little bloke.

In reality, however, we would be better to say, "What a big, strong, powerful, rugged meek fellow." When we identify meekness with being effete, we pervert the virtue.

Meekness is not really possible until power is at stake. We can learn meekness in the company of lions. The mother lion lies quietly with her cubs playing about her. In their weakness they nip each other with full strength. Watching them, we may think they are just playing. They are not playing. They are fighting. They are learning to be full-grown lions. But they do not have the power to hurt each other. They are biting with all their might. But their little jaws are like the pincers of crabs. They nip and pinch. They irritate, but they cannot possibly inflict serious wounds.

Now behold the great lioness with power in her jaws to snap the hind legs of a full-grown impala. She reaches down and picks up her baby cubs in her fearsome mouth. She has the power to snuff out their lives. Yet between her ominous jaws the babies lie quietly and safely in the midst of her power. She, not the cubs, is meek.

Meekness is rarely provoked. It is easily pacified. It is controlled. It is patient. It is easily entreated. It is willing to forgive when forgiveness will earn no reward. Meekness is love in the driver's seat.

When a culture distorts meekness to mean weakness, its leaders grow increasingly ruthless. "Might makes right" becomes the motto of such a culture, and the weak are plowed under. Indeed, the weak in any society depend for protection, not on the mighty, but on the meek. When meekness disappears, the most defenseless elements of the society are at risk.

Meekness is not really possible until power is at stake.

Take, for example, the relationship between mother and child. The infant, born or unborn, is subject to his mother's power. Life and death are in her hands. The argument for abortion in the name of the woman's right to choose could only arise in a cultural atmosphere devoid of meekness. Because modern Western society sees no virtue in meekness, mothers grow more ruthless in their power.

The Meekness of Jesus Christ

Everything was spoken into existence, and nothing that we see was made without the Lord Jesus. Unto Him all things will return. It was appropriate for Him to consider Himself as having full rights in the Godhead. He is the second person of the triune God! Yet, having full authority in the Godhead, He laid all that aside and clothed Himself in mere mortality. Being found in the form of a man, He took upon Himself the likeness of a servant (see Phil. 2:6-7). (The word that is translated "servant" in the KJV might even better be rendered "slave.")

137

Therefore Paul admonishes us to own up to Christ's way of thinking. We are called to embrace His whole approach to living. Christ Jesus laid aside His rights as God to become not only a man but a slave of men. Born in an occupied country under the authority of foreign soldiers, He was crucified by men whom He had created. God, willing to lay aside His authority over the earth and become earth, is meekness perfected.

The Blessings of the Meek

There are great promises for the meek. Miss the virtue and miss the blessings.

Matthew 11:29 is an illuminating passage of Scripture: "Take my yoke upon you, and learn of me; for I am meek and lowly in heart: and ye shall find rest unto your souls."

We must settle ourselves into the double-ox yoke with Jesus. With Jesus on one side and us on the other and the ox yoke securely around our necks, we discover His meekness. When He turns left, we turn left. When He turns right, we turn right. We learn to walk at His pace. We learn to move when He moves and to stand still when He stops. When He pauses, we wait patiently. We fit ourselves to Him. We learn of Him; therefore we learn about Him. Therefore we become like Him. The longer we walk with Him, the more we walk like Him. The longer we talk with Him, the more we talk like Him. Like two old married people, we grow to look more alike.

Second, meekness brings happiness in this life. Meekness makes a man fit to live with because he is not easily threatened by the loss of his power. Without constant striving to gain dominance, the meek reject manipulative tactics.

Meekness makes a man fit to do business. The meek man will not do business out of competitive neurosis. Not needing to "get the upper hand" in every deal, the meek are to be trusted. Therefore, because they are honest, the meek tend to prosper. The meek will be happy in this life not only because they are fit to be with and fit to deal with, but because they are fit to be alone. A man who cannot stand to be alone with himself is a miserable and unhappy person. But a meek man is satisfied with the yoke of Jesus. He is perfectly happy to be alone because he is in fact not alone. He who guides his footsteps also communes with a man in the hidden place.

God, willing to lay aside His authority over the earth and become earth, is meekness perfected.

Third, the meek shall inherit the earth. In Lerner and Loewe's musical comedy *Camelot*, the frustrated knights sarcastically proclaim that the meek don't inherit the earth; they inherit the dirt.[1] The problem is that those erstwhile Knights of the Round Table failed to understand their own words. To inherit means to come into authority, to receive dominance over. It is, in other words, the key to dominion. The passage in Matthew may refer to the earth which God used to form human flesh — our own "earthen vessels" (2 Cor. 4:7). It can mean, therefore, that self-possession, dominion over all hungers and mortal passions, is the inheritance of the meek. The meek have dominion over their own earthen vessels.

There is also a future tense application to the promise. There *is* a new earth coming, an earth so beautiful and so perfect that it is not to be inherited by the grasping power-mongers of this age. This new earth will be so flawless that it is reserved only for the meek.

The knights were wrong. It is not the dirt the meek

inherit. It *is* the earth. After this one is burned away along with its corrupt military, political and economic power systems, the meek shall live and reign with Him eternally.

I was in West Africa some years ago attending a Wycliffe Summer Institute of Linguistics camp. While there, I met an old German missionary.

It is not the dirt the meek inherit. It is the earth.

She was in her seventies, had river blindness and was on her way home to die. In the little place where we stayed, her room was down the hall from mine. Often I would stand at the end of the hall and watch her as she would go down the hallway tracing her hand along the wall. As she would come to a door, she would trace the door, realize what it was, go to the other side and move on.

One day I stopped her in the hallway and introduced myself to her. She spoke a little English, so we were able to share together.

After she went on, an old Ghanaian who was with me said, "Do you know that old lady has single-handedly translated the entire New Testament into two languages? She has two complete New Testaments to her credit. She's one of the greatest translators Wycliffe has ever had. She's contracted river blindness and is going back to Germany to die. She has no family. No one is waiting to greet the plane. She's going home to die."

I got on the plane to go home myself, and I remember picking up the London *Times* and seeing a picture of Col. Muammar Qaddafi as he rode in his car down the streets of the capital city of Libya. You could see the people with their rifles in the air, cheering. Their guns blazed as their warrior chief rode down the middle of the street. There was something in me that flared up. I thought to myself,

Here is a brigand, an absolute criminal, a gangster who is celebrated as a hero by multiplied hundreds of thousands, shooting their rifles in the air and proclaiming him the lord of his country, while this precious, sainted old woman dies in obscurity.

Then the Holy Spirit came to me in that airplane, comforted me and said, "When the rifles of Libya are silent and Qaddafi is answering for his life, she will receive an inheritance incorruptible and undefiled that fadeth not away."

Fourth, according to Psalm 25:9, God will guide the meek in what is right and teach them His way. Because of that the meek live in peace instead of in the world's confusion and turmoil. The meek are submitted to the yoke of God. Resting in His will, they live without all that striving, agonizing, gut-wrenching doubt which owns the minds of the masses.

Judgment for Meekness

God Himself, says Psalm 76:9, will judge and save all the meek of the earth. The meek can rest themselves in the face of injustices now because ultimately God will set it right. I find that when we are the most outraged over injustice, we are most likely to lose touch with meekness. Meekness takes the patient, long-run view of God's justice.

This is not some hoary Old Testament view. Even the book of Revelation says that the blood of the martyrs cries out from underneath the altar. "How long, O God? How long, O God, until You arise and judge the earth?" (see Rev. 6:10).

There is something in us that cries out that the righteousness of God be vindicated in an earth that makes the blood-thirsty tyrant a hero. There is a balance here — on the one hand refusing to turn a blind eye to injustices and on the other becoming complacent. Justice and vengeance are not the same. God has ordained that on this earth civil government bears the sword for the purpose of rendering justice (Rom. 13:1-4). Wrath and eternal justice (vengeance) belong only to God. The spirit of meekness says, I can entrust this to God. Vengeance and wrath are not emotions which humans are capable of handling. The reason God says, "Vengeance is mine," is not because vengeance is wrong. Vengeance is right. It must come. But it must never be in the wrong hands. We are insufficient to the task.

Vengeance in our hands will destroy us. We are not God, and vengeance is a godly thing. Anytime anyone takes vengeance in his own hands, he makes himself as God.

Meekness in Leadership

Meekness at any level will enhance a culture. It is absolutely essential in leadership. The distortion of meekness in the political, military, economic and religious leadership will thoroughly pervert any culture.

Ascending to the throne at his father's death, young Rehoboam sought counsel. To follow Solomon's fame and glory was no easy task for the young king. He needed wisdom.

> And king Rehoboam consulted with the old men, that stood before Solomon his father while he yet lived, and said, How do ye advise that I may answer this people? And they spake unto him, saying, If thou wilt be a servant unto this people this day, and wilt serve them, and answer them, and speak good words to them,

> then they will be thy servants for ever (1 Kin.
> 12:6-7).

The graybeards advised him to meekness and servant-hood as the leader of his nation. The old men understood the virtue of meekness. The young men, however, gave quite different counsel.

> And he said unto them, What counsel give ye that we may answer this people, who have spoken to me, saying, Make the yoke which thy father did put upon us lighter? And the young men that were grown up with him spake unto him, saying, Thus shalt thou speak unto this people that spake unto thee, saying, Thy father made our yoke heavy, but make thou it lighter unto us; thus shalt thou say unto them, My little finger shall be thicker than my father's loins (1 Kin. 12:9-10).

Their blatant appeal to Rehoboam's insecurity won out. The obscene comparison between Rehoboam and his father Solomon did not miss the mark either. It may have been sophomoric and irrational, but it touched the raw nerves of Rehoboam's self-doubts.

The nation shuddered at the new king's first speech. "Solomon, my father, chastised you with whips — *I* will chastise you with scorpions" (see 1 Kin. 12:11b). Rehoboam made it clear that he was no man's servant.

The CEO who wants to lead in the style of Jesus takes upon himself the mantle of meekness. He never asks himself how his employees can further his career. He seeks instead to help every employee fulfill *his* own potential as a human being and a productive member of society.

The meek pastor does not ask himself how his staff, elders and membership can help fulfill his fantasies for ministry. He asks himself, rather, what he can do that will bring *them* into the fullness of the stature of Christ.

The politician who is meek does not ask himself what the people can do to carve him out a niche in history. He seeks some way to bless the least member of his constituency.

There was a city, an ancient and barbaric city, that needed a new king. They called four of their leading citizens and said to each, "We're offering you the opportunity to be king of the city."

The key of the city was placed on a table before each man, one at a time.

The first was a warrior, a brave and courageous warrior whose exploits in battle had won him great fame. They said, "Put both of your hands palm down on the table." The key of the city lay between them.

They said, "If you want to be king badly enough, you would be willing to lose one of your hands."

A man with an axe stood ominously at each end of the table. "If you want the key, you may grasp it," said the people. "But you can only move one of your hands, and the other one will be cut off. If you grasp the key with your right hand, the key is yours, and you will be the king. But you will lose your left."

The warrior reasoned to himself, My right hand is my sword hand; I dare not lose *it*. My right hand is the source of my authority and power.

But he wanted to be king more than anything. He grabbed it with his right hand. Those barbaric citizens cruelly chopped off his left hand and cast him out of the city. "Remnant, you are not worthy to be our king!" they shouted at him.

The second was a philosopher. Not knowing the fate of the warrior, he struggled with the same question. They said to him, in turn, "Choose one." He reasoned within himself, I write with my left hand, and the source of my authority and power is creativity. Therefore I will grasp the key with my left hand and let them chop off my right. They did, indeed, and then cast him out of the city like the warrior. They said, "You are not worthy to be a king."

The third man was the richest merchant in the city. He did not know the fate of the other two. All he saw before him was the golden key and all the riches and power that it implied. His greed consumed him. Not thinking, he clutched the key with both hands and lost both. They cast him handless out of the city.

The fourth was a farmer. With the key between his hands, the question was put to him. He quickly withdrew *both* hands. The farmer explained, "My hands are my only means of service in this cruel world. I will not sacrifice *any* of my ability to grow food for my fellow man merely for the sake of power." Instantly every citizen of the kingdom fell at his feet. They said, "Only one who despises power is worthy to have it." ■

Leaders Without Meekness

There are several types of leaders without meekness. Outwardly they wear all the signs of success, but their virtueless little lives are hidden behind veneers of power.

Type I — King Ahasuerus is unapproachable, infallible and unable to make a mistake. In the book of Esther, anyone approaching this ancient king without being summoned, including his wife, would die if the king did not extend his scepter. By simply sitting motionless, this king killed.

The meek lays down the scepter of authority and

makes himself approachable. The meek leader is able to admit others into his real presence, not sentencing them to the death of separation and seclusion.

The father or husband without meekness is a glacial mountain. He is frozen, distant and silent. Because of fear of rejection, he withdraws into a shell of protection. Any who approach unbidden may die.

The meek leader receives both criticism and compliments with humor and therefore with balance.

Type II is Macho Man. He is threatened by his own inadequacies and fearful that he is not altogether male. Therefore he repeatedly celebrates his maleness. Macho man is constantly seeking to tighten his fragile hold on masculinity by pumping iron at the gym or attending profane poker parties or through sexual adventure. He is constantly reminding himself, I'm a male. I'm a male. I'm a male. That's the reason why there is often a paper-thin membrane separating Macho Man, absorbed with his own well-toned muscles, and the effeminate homosexual.

Type III is Suffering Martyr. He is tired and nearly beaten. He has paid the price for his family. When he is assailed, his authority is threatened or his will is questioned, he is tired, discouraged, unable to respond, but right.

Many actually mistake Suffering Martyr for a man of meekness. In reality he is bankrupt. He has retreated behind a wall of grieved condescension. Suffering Martyr is so right and so far above others that he cannot even attempt to explain his pain and sorrow. It is cowardly and unjust leadership. Even more basically, Suffering Martyr has lost a key element of balanced, mature living and leadership. He has lost his sense of humor.

A sense of humor is not the ability to detect what is funny. A sense of humor is the ability to laugh at oneself. If someone else slips on a banana peel and you laugh, that has nothing to do with your sense of humor. If *you* slip on a banana peel and laugh, you have a sense of humor.

A meek man will laugh at his own pratfall. Suffering Martyr sees *nothing* funny about his plight. The meek leader receives both criticism and compliments with humor and therefore with balance.

Meekness and Rebellion

Chafing under the leadership of their brother Moses, Miriam and Aaron began to reason in the flesh and not in the Spirit. Surely Moses did not have a corner on the God market. They were as mature as he. In fact, when Moses had fled to Midian, they had remained in Egypt. They had out-suffered Moses if nothing else. Then there was this matter of the foreign woman. Moses' gentile wife galled them.

Aaron was a prophet. And Miriam — was she excluded because she was a woman? God could not be so unjust. No, *Moses*, not God, was their complaint. They were as good as he, and they wanted their fair share of the power.

Finally, in Numbers 12, their inner rebellion burst into the open. Comparing their ministry and spirituality with his, Aaron and Miriam laid at least partial claim on leadership.

> Now the man Moses was very meek, above all
> the men which were upon the face of the earth
> (Num. 12:3).

Because of his meekness, Moses never once struggled to retain power. He left it to God. Moses did not speak for Moses — *God* spoke for Moses.

> And the Lord spake suddenly unto Moses, and unto Aaron, and unto Miriam, Come out ye three unto the tabernacle of the congregation. And they three came out. And the Lord came down in the pillar of the cloud, and stood in the door of the tabernacle, and called Aaron and Miriam: and they both came forth. And he said, Hear now my words: If there be a prophet among you, I the Lord will make myself known unto him in a vision, and will speak unto him in a dream.
>
> My servant Moses is not so, who is faithful in all mine house. With him will I speak mouth to mouth, even apparently, and not in dark speeches; and the similitude of the Lord shall he behold: wherefore then were ye not afraid to speak against my servant Moses? And the anger of the Lord was kindled against them; and he departed. And the cloud departed from off the tabernacle; and, behold, Miriam became leprous, white as snow: and Aaron looked upon Miriam, and, behold, she was leprous. And Aaron said unto Moses, Alas, my lord, I beseech thee, lay not the sin upon us, wherein we have done foolishly, and wherein we have sinned.
>
> Let her not be as one dead, of whom the flesh is half consumed when he cometh out of his mother's womb. And Moses cried unto the Lord, saying, Heal her now, O God, I beseech thee (Num. 12:4-13).

148

The first time Moses speaks in the entire event is to intercede for Miriam's healing.

Moses did not spring to the defense of his own ministry. He did not struggle to hold on to the chains of authority. He simply said, "God gave me this. If God wants me to have it, it is God's business. If God no longer wants me to have it, that is God's business too." That is the spirit of meekness.

The Hebrew word for meekness has an intriguing alternate translation. It is "disinterested." Read Numbers 12:3 that way.

> Now the man Moses was very [disinterested],
> above all the men which were upon the face of
> the earth.

Moses said, "I have no vested interest in this matter. This is the Lord's business. These are God's people. It is God's tabernacle. It is God's power. It is God's glory. It is God's nation. It is God's business. I am personally *disinterested*. God can do whatever He wants."

Aaron and Miriam were murmuring and grasping. The question was one of authority and power.

To the arrogant, self-centered husband claiming to be "the head of the household," God says, Learn the meekness of Moses. As the God-appointed leader of a nation, he wanted the last little baby across the Red Sea, dryshod. He was infinitely concerned that each of his people live in the holiness of God. But, concerning who was to be boss, Moses was flatly disinterested.

The pastor who constantly stands in the pulpit crying, "I am the boss. I am the boss," has missed the whole meaning of pastor as servant. The servant-pastor says to his people, "What I want for you is what God wants for you. My only purpose in being in this ministry is for you to know all that God has for you."

It is in a great part a lack of meekness in leadership which causes strikes that bankrupt industries. The CEO says to the rank and file, "Make my dreams come true! Work harder. Make me rich."

The union boss shouts, "We want control! Power to the union!"

It is the lack of meekness in leadership on both sides that will bring the industry to its knees.

The leadership style of Moses was quite different. His thinking was, You want to be the boss? *Be* the boss. But *God* said, I choose Moses.

The Great Qualities of the Meek Leader

First, his achievements may be great, but they appear not to be his alone. *Second*, his transforming influence may touch many, but those thus touched do not learn to depend on him. *Third*, his subordinates admire his virtues greatly but are free to explore their own strengths without fear of his domination. *Fourth*, the meek leader is not afraid of the responsibility of leadership, but his authority does not dictate to him who he is. Rather his meekness dominates the demonstration of his authority for the good of those whom he serves.

The apostles asked, "Lord, who will be the greatest in Your kingdom?" And Jesus gave no answer. Instead, He took a basin of water and wrapped a towel around His waist and began to wash their feet. Later the might of pagan Rome unleashed a holocaust against Christ's followers. It was that abiding memory of a God-man willing to wash their feet that gave them the power to topple an empire.

IX

REVERENCE

The Perspective of Worthship

The horrifying obscenity that erupted from his little son's mouth so flabbergasted David Whiteside that he was absolutely speechless for several seconds. They stared at each other. The father in unblinking, shocked amazement searched the lad's face for some explanation. He saw not the slightest trace of remorse or even fear. Young, six-year-old Marty for his part saw the startled horror in his father's eyes and wondered at it. What could be wrong? he asked himself. They seemed to be having a good time.

It was the gay, sparkling laughter of Irene Whiteside that finally broke the spell. Gales of her sweet, unfeigned, flowing laughter so spilled out upon the two males that in only seconds they were swept along in its inebriating tide.

Soon the three of them were laughing and rolling about on the carpet. It was a wild scene of intimacy and fun. Little Marty Whiteside did not understand what had precipitated the near collision. But he had felt it deeply, and his laughter was nearly hysterical at the relief. The parents laughed for a reason they did not fully understand, but the moment was warmly consistent with their family's fun-loving informality, and they silently agreed not to make a big deal about it.

"Now, Marty, don't *ever* say that again," Whiteside finally admonished when the ruckus on the carpet ended in soft fatigue. "That's *not* the way we talk around here."

Marty had no idea what his father meant, but the reassuring smile and his father's giant hand tousling his wheat-colored hair told him it was all right. Marty had already learned at six to discern when his father was "just saying stuff" and when he "meant business." He could tell this was the former.

"Yes, sir," said the boy as he seized his father's neck, hoping to incite the happy riot again.

Later that night after Marty's bedtime, David and Irene Whiteside reflected on the incident as they sat idly watching TV.

"I'm sorry I laughed," Irene chuckled. "I absolutely couldn't help myself."

"Oh, it's OK," he assured her, patting her arm gently. "I know how you felt. I couldn't help thinking how the deacons at the church would have felt. That's what I was laughing at."

At that Irene almost doubled over in laughter. "Oh, my

Lord, can you imagine if he ever said that in front of old Miss Louise?"

"What I wonder is, where did he hear that?" David asked.

"Oh, God only knows," his wife said. "You can't protect them from the world."

"Yeah, that's right," David muttered, turning his eyes back to the TV.

Irene shrugged and sighed. She hated this crazy show. She really did not see what her husband enjoyed in it. The skit was about God and the devil. She supposed the idea of God as a black lesbian *was* funny in a sort of off-the-wall way, but she didn't really like it. Something about the show made her uncomfortable.

"Well," she said, "I'm going up to bed."

"OK," he said, laughing at the ludicrous skit on the TV. "I'll be up soon."

"You'd better," she warned gently. "You know you don't preach as well when you're tired."

"I know," he said. "I'm coming. I just want to see this. This is a scream! It ought to be required viewing for all those fuddy-duddies I pastor."

"David!" Irene said. "Don't talk — "

"Oh, all right," he said. "I won't! I won't! But the thought of Miss Louise dying and appearing before God only to find out God is a black lesbian with a white woman live-in — well, it's just too rich."

"Come to bed soon, honey," chuckled Irene. "Church is early, and you know you like to look fresh. By the way, I got your robe cleaned. You'll look so handsome." ■

Civilizations are profoundly shaped by what they revere. As merit is assigned to things, persons and institutions, a society determines whether or not its thread of virtue will hold.

A society that revered murderers above doctors, for example, would surely become increasingly violent. However, when the contrast is so obvious as that between doctors and murderers, the point is hardly subtle. It becomes a bit less apparent, however, when the choice is between doctors who do murder (that is, a "successful" abortionist) and sewer workers who do *not* do murder.

Modern American humor is frighteningly irreverent.

If virtue is reverenced, virtue increases. If virtueless success or characterless talent is held aloft, the thread begins to unravel. If impious rock stars are admired above pious clergymen, the thread is stressed to the breaking point. Of course, the snap comes when blatant irreverence is touted as a virtue.

Modern American humor is frighteningly irreverent. Irreverence has become a theatrical virtue. In the light of the whole counsel of God we *must* recapture the sober reality that there are some things that are *not* funny. They are not funny to God. They must not be funny to us. Americans tend to say, "This movie was blasphemous and wicked and horrible and murderous and pornographic, but it was *so* funny."

In an interview, a certain TV performer on a popular comedy show explained the huge success of the program. He said in part it had been the talent of the people involved. But, more than that, he explained, "Our success came from our determination that nothing, absolutely nothing, was sacred." That "nothing is sacred" may well prove to be the epitaph of the West.

There are some things that *are* sacred. There are likewise some things that just are not funny. To jest of those things which are high and holy is to intrude dangerously on the things of God.

A massive advertising campaign was used to promote a recent motion picture. Its producers proudly proclaimed the picture as being "wildly irreverent — the 'must see' picture of the summer." It is frightening enough when we somehow justify entertainment despite its irreverence. But when a movie's irreverence is its major recommendation for our society, sin has become virtue, and virtue has become sin.

Beside the extremely popular movie star whose blatant irreverence has propelled him into stardom, the ruddy-cheeked Cub Scout with his well-scrubbed little hand raised in a vow of reverence is ridiculous. In fact, in a well-funded multimedia assault the reverent little scout may be made to look more sinister than silly. His uniformed, clean-cut, conservative posture in the hands of Norman Lear can be made to look like the Hitler Youth.

What is revered and how such reverence is demonstrated is crucial to a society. In other words, appropriate objects of reverence must be chosen and assigned their proper values. Then appropriate means of demonstrating that reverence must be found.

Lecturing in African classrooms, I discovered that the students there stand beside their desk when their teachers enter the room. I have often wondered if such respect for teachers can ever again be taught in American classrooms.

Many years ago I also taught for a while in Washington, D.C. That job afforded me the unhappy experience of escorting a group of junior high students to the National Gallery of Art. I found the experience not unlike attending a debutante ball with the Hell's Angels. The reason it was so exasperating was not merely their bad behavior. It was rather the painful sense of casting pearls before swine. I kept asking, "Don't you understand? This is a Renoir."

They would answer, "Hey, Renoir ain't nothing in my book. Do they have a sports section?"

They cared nothing for Gauguin or Van Gogh. Michelangelo was a nobody. They wanted action photos of basketball stars. The beauty or history of various works was totally wasted on them.

What irritated me was not that we had different tastes. It was their belligerent lack of appreciation. They refused to see that great art is worth esteeming more highly than bubble gum.

This is not to advocate that supercilious condescension that makes highbrow artistic tastes the ultimate virtue. That is not what I am talking about at all. I simply refer to a modern failure to understanding proper worth. In our current informality, there is a danger of losing all sense of propriety. The greater danger may be the loss of the humility sufficient to see that a thing is simply wonderful, that it is worthy of my taking notice.

The risk of being stuffy and overly formal is real. But the risk on the other side of losing respect, dignity and reverence altogether is far greater.

Reverence is directly related to humility. There is nothing more obnoxious than arrogant teenage brats who are bored with life.

Our society has cultivated a deliberate boredom. We have largely lost our ability to see the wonder and beauty in anything. Many American teenagers spend their lives bored with everything. As a result they have become monumentally boring.

One thing that frightens me greatly about America's youth and their cultivated taste for boredom is their apparent inability to be impressed. There are certain things that simply demand a response. It is arrogant and self-centered to stand for the first time at the foot of Mt.

Fuji and say, "Ho hum, it's about what I thought." How infinitely more interesting life is with a person who is unafraid to say, "I never dreamed it would be so beautiful!"

I was with some businessmen at a great luxury hotel where I was to speak. The hotel was an absolute wonder. In the lobby was one of the largest indoor atriums I have ever seen. It was a virtual tropical rainforest. Above it all the guests strolled on elevated walkways affording beautiful vistas in every direction. It was fabulous!

One evening as I walked with several men from the convention, I was extolling its virtues. After a few moments of my oohs and ahs, one of my embarrassed friends said, "You know, Dr. Rutland, people are going to think you've never seen anything like this before."

One thing that frightens me greatly about America's youth...is their apparent inability to be impressed.

I said, "I haven't! I am impressed with this hotel. Aren't you?"

They sheepishly — and only after furtive glances about — admitted they were.

There is something arrogant about a person who refuses to be impressed with anything. We must teach the young a sense of wonder. There are certain things in the face of which I simply ought to be astonished.

The parents of just such a bored eleven-year-old took him to the Grand Canyon. He seemed unable to be impressed with anything. Standing at a certain overlook, the boy finally seemed awed at one of the guide's statistics.

"This is a half-mile straight down? Wow!" the boy exclaimed.

"Yes," answered the guide patiently.

"You're sure?" the boy pressed him.

"Yes. That is a half-mile straight drop," the ranger assured him.

"Wow!" the boy kept saying. "Wow!"

That night when their son was sound asleep, the happy parents crept into his room to read his diary entry for the day. They were confident that at last the boy had been impressed with *something*.

The lad's diary entry read: "Wow! Today I could spit a half-mile." ■

The virtuous have things, people and God in right perspective. Integrity and character are the result of correctly estimating worth. A man without virtue is doomed by his own inability to estimate value rightly. Reverence is the virtue of correctly perceiving true worth.

In the classical, antiquated English use, reverence is a verb, meaning to bow before, to make obeisance. It is frequently used in that sense in the Old Testament.

To reverence is to show respect, to accord some exalted or sacred status. That respect may be at a level which, depending on culture, may require a bow or a special signal such as a military salute. To reverence the flag, one places hand on heart. To show proper respect may mean to stand silently. Still again, reverence may simply be a matter of the heart and require no outward demonstration.

Only reverencing some things outside myself tears my eyes off my own importance. When I cultivate the virtue of reverence, of right estimation, I cut away at my natural tendency to make myself the center of all things. The perspective that reverence returns to my life is not only spiritually important. It is crucial to emotional well-being.

A certain woman in a state of depression went to a

psychiatrist. At the end of the six weeks of $150-an-hour sessions, the doctor said, "I'm going to write a prescription now that will cure you."

He wrote this on the prescription pad: "Go to Niagara Falls, New York. Check into a motel. Leave your suitcase. Go to the falls. Stand on the bottom observation platform and stare up at Niagara Falls for five hours. Repeat this every day for a week, and you'll be cured."

"You quack!" she howled. "I pay you almost a thousand dollars for six sessions, and you tell me to go stare at a waterfall. What can you be thinking of?"

> *Reverence is the virtue of correctly perceiving true worth.*

"Lady," he explained, "I have met with you for six weeks at $150 an hour. I told you to talk to me about anything you wanted. All you talk about is yourself; *your* dreams, *your* nightmares, *your* worries, *your* fears, *your* past, *your* background. The only thing you need to get well is to see something bigger than you are." ■

A great contributing factor to the increasing madness of Western culture is the decline of reverence. The tide of insanity rising currently in the West is in great part due to the fact that when man is at the center of his own life, neurosis, fear, violence and outright insanity result. Let that madness become endemic in any society and the thread becomes a filament trying to support an elephantine carcass of dead weight.

The question, of course, is what to reverence. Statesmanship is the mastery of statecraft. Churchmanship is the proper stewarding of resources in the activities of the church. Likewise, to assign worth properly is *worth*ship. From just this combination of words we get the single word "worship."

As we individuals and societies assign worth, we order our priorities, arrange our values and determine our virtues. Worthship ranges then from its lowest expression (mere respect) all the way to its highest — what I worship as being worth my ultimate devotion; what I worship as God.

He that esteems righteousness too lowly and he that esteems unrighteousness too highly are both an abomination to God.

Admiration of particular individuals is one aspect of reverence. It is not wrong to admire certain qualities, abilities or achievements of individuals. But we must be constantly vigilant against admiring men or wickedness.

Proverbs 17:15 says, "He that justifieth the wicked, and he that condemneth the just, even they both are abomination to the Lord."

He that esteems righteousness too lowly and he that esteems unrighteousness too highly are both an abomination to God. To idolize immoral movie stars, rock stars and ball players is to revere the unrighteous. We should respect and admire achievements which are made in any field of endeavor. Yet issues of character remain infinitely more important.

Years ago a baseball player achieved a great statistical landmark in his career. My little son read the newspaper accounts with fevered excitement. "Oh, Daddy, look at what this guy has done! I would love to be like him," he sighed.

I took Travis up on my lap and explained my convictions to him. "Travis, I understand what you're saying. There's never been a little boy who didn't want his name on the front page of the sports section. I understand that. But if you grow up to be like that man, Daddy couldn't stand it. I simply could not stand it. That man has been sued for paternity suits. He's a lying, conniving, hard-drinking, hard-swearing, corrupt human being. He can swing a baseball bat, but he is a failure as a man. His life is out of control. The Bible says that a man whose life is out of control is like a city with the walls broken down."

I explained, "Travis, it's OK for you to say, 'I'd like to bat like him.' But don't ever admire him. He is *not* an admirable man."

That conversation stayed with my son. Years later that same man got involved in a scandalous illegal situation, and Travis remembered my words.

When the front pages announced the grim tragedy, Travis said to me, "You remember what you told me about that man? You were right, Dad. You were sure right."

Well, of course, I was thrilled! It was the first time I had been right about anything in many, many years. But beyond that, I was glad for Travis and for society.

We must get a right perspective on those things that are worthy. We must also get a right perspective on those things that are unworthy. We must see beyond popularity with a sinful world. We must see beyond screaming crowds. We must see things as they really are. We must see beyond wealth. We must see beyond prosperity. We must be able to estimate things at the level of reality. Remember, that man who honors the dishonorable and he who esteems the righteous too lowly are both an abomination to God.

There is a passage in Leviticus 19 which gives some insights into levels of reverence.

> Ye shall not eat any thing with the blood: neither shall ye use enchantment, nor observe

times. Ye shall not round the corners of your heads, neither shalt thou mar the corners of thy beard. Ye shall not make any cuttings in your flesh for the dead, nor print any marks upon you: I am the Lord. Do not prostitute thy daughter, to cause her to be a whore; lest the land fall to whoredom, and the land become full of wickedness. Ye shall keep my sabbaths, and reverence my sanctuary: I am the Lord. Regard not them that have familiar spirits, neither seek after wizards, to be defiled by them: I am the Lord your God. Thou shalt rise up before the hoary head [gray-haired man], and honour the face of the old man, and fear thy God: I am the Lord (Lev. 19:26-32).

Notice the flow of the passage. The text has to do with assigning worth and establishing levels of reverence.

Levels of Reverence in Leviticus 19

1. Reverence life and the body: Do not eat blood. Do not cut your hair or beard in bizarre pagan fashions. Do not cut or tattoo your flesh.

2. Reverence relationships and sex: Do not dishonor or use your family. Do not make sex pornographic. Do not sell your bodies, nor those of others.

3. Reverence the things of God: Do not make light of those things which pertain unto God.

4. Reverence age: Do not do violence or show disrespect to elders. Their wisdom comes from God. They show the way ahead of you.

Notice how many of the exhortations end with the words I AM THE LORD. In other words, the ultimate worth of God is the explanation of all respect and reverence. The body is important and to be respected BE-CAUSE GOD MADE IT! Respect the aged because God is their maker and judge and because they are, in His established order, closer to entering His presence than younger people are.

Western contempt and even hatred for the elderly is a monstrosity of irreverence. The society which despises its elderly hates both its past *and* its future. A generation that denies respect to its elderly and protection to its unborn has denied God's ownership upon human life. Weakness and frailty become the signal to attack. Affluent mothers turn hired assassins loose on the fruit of their wombs, and rebellious teens mock and mug their grandparents in the parks.

Look back at the passage from Leviticus. What is the purpose of including the oddly placed reference to witchcraft in the midst of a teaching about respect and reverence?

There is a connection between common irreverence which breeds disrespect and the profound spiritual arrogance of witchcraft. Out of rebellion comes witchcraft. Call it by any name that pleases fashion, but the elements of the New Age movement are nothing new. It is simply witchcraft born of rebellious irreverence. The New Age movement is the result of our culture having wrongly estimated the things of God.

Humility and gratitude are the enabling catalysts of a true spirit of reverence. When men see themselves in right perspective with God and the things of God, they see who they are in Him and have a proper estimation of themselves. In right relation to Him, we find humility.

Respect for elders, dignitaries and authority is not merely a social issue, nor is it merely a matter of changing manners. It is a spiritual issue. The spirit of rebellion is the malevolent cousin of witchcraft.

Respect for the office must be taught. It is important for students to know that teachers are to be respected. They may not be the greatest people in the world, but they are the teachers. The principal is to be respected. Elders are to be respected. Presidents, police, mayors and aldermen are to be respected. The respect is for the office. Even if I disagree with the man, I *must* respect the office.

Only the understanding of reverencing because of the authorship of God lends meaning to life and relationships. Without a biblical view of reverence, the most shallow and superficial things in life may be afforded huge respect. Meanwhile things, people, offices and ideas of monumental importance are ground under foot like garbage. All too often there is a problem in knowing whether society is making a thing too important or making a thing altogether unimportant.

For example, reverence for sex is a deeply confused issue. Even among those opposed to pornography and prostitution there are many who do not understand why these are evil. Pornography does not say that sex is so important that we can put it above God. That is a common misconception about the "philosophy" of pornography. That is not what pornography is about. Pornography says sex is so low, so mean, so miserable, so common, so animal that we may treat it any way we want. Pornography is based on the premise that sex is unimportant. The biblical response is not that sex is so dirty that we dare not mention it in church. The reason pornography is wrong is not because sex is wrong. The reason pornography is wrong is because it makes sex too unimportant. Pornography does not reverence sex. The Bible does. Sex is important because it was made by God. God created sex; Hugh Hefner did not. And God was in a nifty mood that day. Sex is a good thing. It is a holy thing.

The book of Proverbs says there are four things in

creation that are absolutely wonderful. What are those things? A graceful ship in the sea, the majestic aerodynamics of an eagle, a snake moving so effortlessly, so silently upon a stone. The writer innocently marvels at such wonders of God. Finally he mentions sex: "the way of a man with a maid." That, says Proverbs, is just wonderful, full of wonder, awesome, beautiful, important, holy.

Even if I disagree with the man, I must respect the office.

We must reverence life itself. The reason abortion is wrong is because life is the fundamental reflection of its Creator. To do away with life selfishly because we have our perspective of worth out of order is to touch the apple of God's eye. If I have esteemed life correctly, life will be reverenced over convenience, over finances, over reputation, over relationships. Life is holy because God made life. When self-interest is worth more than life, society goes insane.

Psalm 89:7-11 is a magnificent insight:

> God is greatly to be feared in the assembly of the saints, and to be had in reverence of all them that are about him. O Lord God of hosts, who is a strong Lord like unto thee? or to thy faithfulness round about thee? Thou rulest the raging of the sea: when the waves thereof arise, thou stillest them. Thou hast broken Rahab in pieces, as one that is slain; thou hast scattered thine enemies with thy strong arm. The heavens are thine, the earth also is thine: as for the world and the fulness thereof, thou hast founded them.

In these words we see that in reverencing God, the world, creation, the whole natural order, the cosmos comes into its proper perspective. The world now makes sense because it is made by God. I now make sense because I am made by God. Life has meaning because life was made by God. Birth has meaning. Death has meaning. Precious in the sight of God is the death of His saints. Everything is restored to order. There is discipline. There is creativity. There is order in the universe.

When men and nations drift into irreverence, the very reason for living is lost. Insanity awaits when the thread of reverence snaps. When I see God as worthy, my sense of worthship is restored. When my sense of worthship is restored, my longing to worship comes again.

If I have set those things on high, even creation, even the world, even the universe, the whole cosmos — if I set those on high, my reverence turns to madness and madness to despair. The Bible is perfectly clear. This world and the heavens that we see will burn up as with fire. If I reverence that which will disappear, I make myself temporary.

Many years ago my family was driving through north Mexico on a mission trip. In the middle of the night on a lonely highway a herd of cows suddenly appeared in the road. I stopped to let them get across, but another car filled with men shot around us and hit the cattle full speed. One of those cows was killed instantly. The men tumbled out of their car and stared down at the dead beast. In a few moments they jumped back in their car and sped away into the night.

From the back seat our little boy said, "Dad, remember when we were in India how the people reverenced the cattle?"

"Yes," I said. "I remember that."

He said, "Man, I don't want a God that can be killed

by a carload of men."

If I have fixed my ultimate reverence on that which cannot be shaken away, then when that which is shaken away is gone, my highest pinnacle of reverence remains.

Let us have grace by which we may serve God acceptably, not like rebellious, arrogant, self-centered fifth-graders in the National Gallery of Art throwing spit wads at a Renoir. But staring up at the majesty of heaven, let us cry, "Our God is an awesome God," acceptably, with reverence and with godly fear, for our God is a consuming fire.

Heavenly Father, teach us to estimate things aright. Teach us, O Lord, that which is worthy, not to esteem too highly those things that are unworthy, neither to admire that which is despicable in Your sight, lest we become an abomination. God forbid.

Lord, teach us to reverence those things which are precious in Your sight, and teach us to reverence You above all. God, teach us the perspective of worthship. Teach us what is worthy and worthy to be praised.

God, we praise You. We esteem You more highly than all of these, yea, even than ourselves. Nothing I desire compares with You. We reverence You. We exalt You. We reverence You in our hearts with fear. Amen.

X

GRATITUDE

The Celebration of Grace

The books in the Homer Smith series are among the better ones ever written.[1] Homer Smith is an itinerant black carpenter from the Southern part of the United States. The most famous of these is *The Lilies of the Field*, immortalized in the cinema by Sidney Poitier, who won an academy award for best actor in 1963 for his role in that film.

Homer Smith is not a particularly educated man, but he is a Christian man with a great deal of wisdom. In *The Lilies of the Field* the other main figure of the story is a

German Roman Catholic Mother Superior who is shepherding a small band of four or five nuns in the desert of New Mexico. Hoping to build a church there in the desert, this curmudgeonly old nun is working her fingers to the bone and praying that God will somehow send her a means to get her chapel built. When Homer Smith drives up in his battered station wagon, she is convinced he is the instrument of God. The crotchety old German nun badgers, cajoles, coaxes and tricks Homer Smith into building her church.

You're supposed to spend the rest of your life saying "thank you."

Despite all that, however, she will not tell Smith "thank you." Near the end of the book, by the use of an English lesson, Homer Smith is able to trick that old nun into saying "thank you." For the first time in her life, to man, woman or child, she says, "Thank you." She finds it a jolting experience!

We have been taught successfully as Western Christians that gratitude is among the very highest virtues. Furthermore, gratitude is actually synonymous with the deepest, most profound elements of scriptural holiness. It is of that spiritual universe which includes humility and contentment and praise. Gratitude is diametrically opposed to pride.

Some years ago I came in contact with a teenager who had been raised by his grandparents from infancy. The boy's father had been killed in an automobile accident, and subsequently his mother disappeared. They obviously had been doing all they knew how to for him at great sacrifice to themselves. It is difficult for anyone to raise a teenager, and people in their sixties and seventies ought not to have to go through it a second time around.

For several years he rewarded them with unfathomable rebellion, anger and sin. He simply made that old couple miserable. Finally I could stand it no more. I took him aside and said, "Remember when they took you in. You could have gone to an orphanage. You could have been a ward of the court. Your mother disappeared, your father is dead, and these kind people, your grandparents, took you in. They got up with you in the middle of the night. They changed your diapers, fed you and clothed you. They raised you at sacrifice to themselves. Nobody would have blamed them if they had said, 'We just can't handle it at our age.' "

He replied bitterly, "Do you think this is the first time I've ever thought of all that? I know what they've done. But what am I supposed to do, spend the rest of my life saying 'thank you'?"

Well — yes! Yes! A thousand times *yes*! You're supposed to spend the rest of your life saying "thank you." Everyone is. That is what real life is, an expression of gratitude to God. *Yes*, we are supposed to spend the rest of our lives, every waking moment, saying "thank you." That is what Paul the apostle said. "I consider myself to be in debt, both to the Greek and to the non-Greek. I am indebted to the whole world. I am in debt to *God*!" (see Rom. 1:14).

I often consider my own life. Who am I to preach the unsearchable riches of Christ? These are the same feet that hurried to do sin. These hands were covered with blood. Single-handedly I very nearly destroyed my family, my soul and my sanity. This is the same mouth that uttered blasphemies. God scooped me up out of the gutters of the universe, hosed me down, filled me with the Holy Spirit and gave me back my soul and my sanity. He gave me another chance with my family and then allowed me the privilege to preach the Word of His kingdom. Amazing! Yes. Yes, the rest of my life *is* a "thank you."

Now the reason that boy did not want to accept the fact that *his* life ought to be lived out as a "thank you" is because that implies some sense of responsibility. What he wanted to be free from was the responsibility to, in any way, pay some of it back. He was a perfect example of the self-centered, spoiled brats of the Western hemisphere. What ingrates, those of phenomenal affluence who think that somehow or other they deserve it all.

Ingratitude is, in general, not a sin of the poor, but of the rich. And we are rich. Look at us. A kid who has never had anything and has no hope of having anything, who wakes up cold every morning of his life in a little tar paper shack, is likely to be grateful for the apple he gets for Christmas. But the kid who wakes up every morning in a $350,000 house and who has never worked a day in his life, who puts hundreds of dollars' worth of clothes on his well-scrubbed back every morning and is driven to a private school (that somebody else is paying for) complains about a personal computer for Christmas because it does not have the kind of software he wanted.

I remember the last Christmas I spent in Ghana in West Africa. I was staying in the home of a college president. He was a sophisticated, urbane, educated Ghanaian trapped in a nation on the brink of a nightmare.

In 1980 there was nothing in Ghana. The borders were closed. The shelves of the stores were empty. The people were literally starving to death. Christmas Eve was the birthday of the eldest son. The boy was a senior student at his father's college. No one had a single present to give him. Nothing.

I myself had little with me. I was actually living as they were living, but I wanted to give that boy something for his birthday. I took a used T-shirt out of my luggage, washed it, folded it, put it in a box with an American ten-dollar bill and wrapped it with plain brown paper.

At supper, I handed the boy his one modest gift. I tell you, if I live to be one hundred I will never forget seeing that college senior weeping with gratitude over a used T-shirt and a ten-dollar bill. It made me ashamed.

> The horseleach hath two daughters, crying, Give, give. There are three things that are never satisfied, yea, four things say not, It is enough: The grave; and the barren womb; the earth that is not filled with water; and the fire that saith not, It is enough (Prov. 30:15-16).

The daughters of the horseleach are never satisfied, and they never say "thank you." They continue to demand more and more blood. Never satiated, never grateful, never content, their possessive lust is a bottomless pit.

Ingratitude is a curse to everyone it touches, and it quickly becomes a habit of life. The child taken for ice cream complains because there are no chocolate sprinkles on top. Nothing is quite right, never satisfying and never quite enough. Parents save and sacrifice to take their kids to Disney World, and the children think that somehow that is their just due in life. It never dawns on them that their parents are spending one of the worst vacations of their entire lives just for the kids to have fun. The kids never seem to consider that this is something for which they actually ought to be grateful.

The parents pay some exorbitant entry price to a theme park. They pay five dollars for a hot dog that tastes like sawdust and then stand in the hot sun and eat it. They go on rides that make them wish they were dead and say to themselves the whole time, "I am *paying* people to do this to me!" At the end of the day the parents are exhausted and dead broke. But it's worth it; the children are happy. But the children complain because their parents won't take them to the movies on the way home.

The child of God, at some point, must be able to say to those around him, This is more than I deserve. This is perfect, Dad. Not, This will do. Not, OK, I guess. But, Thanks — this is perfect, and I do *not* deserve perfect.

Recently a seminary student whom I love called to say he wanted to come over in the afternoon and visit. He said, "I want you to meet my girlfriend. I'm going to bring her over too."

I said, "Great, bring her. I'd love to meet her."

He said, "We'll come as soon as we can. Her dad is washing her car." Is this girl crippled? No, she's perfectly healthy, and her dad is out in the driveway washing her car.

I did not have the nerve, but I wanted to ask that girl a few questions. When she got in that beautiful new car, which he paid for and now washes for her, and when she drove out of the driveway, did she say, "Daddy, you're *wonderful*! You're *really* wonderful! Daddy, I love you. I appreciate you"?

I could not but wonder if she merely offered a vague wave of her hand and shouted, "Thanks, Dad," to no one in particular as she roared away.

Ingratitude is actually an expression of selfishness. Ingratitude is infinitely more concerned with self than with the feelings of others who have given.

I remember a funeral I preached a few years ago. It was one of the really discouraging moments of my ministry. A lovely Christian woman, an elderly lady, had died suddenly and left behind a husband who was really not very strong in the Lord. He was not much of a Christian and only attended the church a few times.

The casket was literally blanketed in the most beautiful roses I have ever seen in my life. I commented to the husband, "Sir, I have never seen roses like these. These are beautiful."

He said, "You know, preacher, Margaret loved roses. She was a real sentimental sort of woman. She always wanted me to buy her roses. 'Buy me some roses — buy me roses,' she always used to say."

"Well," he explained, "I'm not really into that sort of thing very much. I never did. I guess I just didn't want to waste money and time on stuff like that."

"But," he said brightly, his moist eyes shining, "I'm making it up to her now."

Ingratitude is infinitely more concerned with self than with the feelings of others who have given.

The fool! She could not even smell them. She could not even see them. He was not making it up to her. He was pouring salve on his own conscience.

Husband, buy her the roses *now*. Don't lean over a cold corpse and say words you meant to say before. "Oh, honey, I think you're wonderful!" Tell her now!

Children, listen. Do not face the day that your mother calls you in and says, "Daddy isn't coming home from work. Something terrible happened at the office," only to realize that you never said, "Thanks, Dad."

Don't get to be forty before you suddenly realize that the clothes you've always worn did not magically get washed. I do not know who I thought was washing my clothes when I was a teenager. The only thing I knew was that they appeared in my chest of drawers every week. *Now* I realize that the pixies were not in there doing the

175

laundry. I did not deserve a mother who washed my clothes till I graduated from high school. I do not deserve the wife who does it now. I am grateful.

There are American teens who would rather stay home from school than show up in discount-store tennis shoes. Life's critical issue in the West has become the brand name on our tennis shoes. But in Cambodia there are teens today who pray, "O God, just once before I die, could I wear a pair of shoes? Any kind of shoes?"

This is not to heap on guilt. It is rather to say that we must awaken to the reality that we are in debt. We are the richest, most powerful, most prosperous, most educated, cleanest, healthiest people who have ever been on the face of the earth. And we are often the most selfish, self-centered, ungrateful people who have ever lived.

All ingratitude is basically ingratitude to God. God blesses us with health, happiness and the joy of children. But we get angry because we are not the president of Ford Motor Company. We pray for a job and then sulk with God because it does not pay what someone else's pays. There are men in this country right now who would give anything in the world just to work. A woman prays for a new house and then gets angry at God because she has to clean it. A single woman prays and prays and prays to catch a husband and then gets angry at God because he's not perfect.

We are seldom just plain, bottom-line grateful with God. God gives us the strawberry sundae, and we are angry because it does not have whipped cream. He gives us the whipped cream, and we are angry because it does not have a cherry on top. At some point we must dare to break the chains of the spirit of the horseleach and say, It is *enough*. Can we ever say, I am content with this. It is more than I deserve?

I believe that gratitude as well as ingratitude can become a habit of life. We can begin to see everything that happens to us as an opportunity to praise God.

I remember hearing Leonard Ravenhill tell of a minister visiting a very horrible insane asylum in the United Kingdom sometime in the early part of the twentieth century. It was a terrible place.

As the minister walked in the front door, a man in a second-story window pressed his head through the bars and shouted down to the visitor below, "Have you thanked God today?"

"I have," answered the pastor.

The man said, "Aye, but have you thanked Him for your sanity?"

We must get specific with God. Instead of complaining about the rain, thank God that you are alive.

Can we ever say, I am content with this. It is more than I deserve?

Instead of complaining about your husband, thank God you are not lonely. Instead of complaining about having to wear this or that kind of shirt, thank God you have a shirt.

Some time ago I played basketball with some pastors in Atlanta. We had a great time. When we finished, we knelt down to pray. There on the polished gym floor, I thought, Here I am playing basketball in an air-conditioned gymnasium while there are men who are infinitely more deserving and more righteous than I who are right at this very moment leading their families through deserts and jungles. They watch as their babies die of starvation. They weep and pray to God that they can find a refuge camp before the soldiers find them. And I have time to play basketball so I will lose weight.

Suddenly I was overwhelmed with gratitude. I wanted nothing except to praise Him and thank Him.

Gratitude is a way of life. It is the open hand instead of the clenched fist. It is saying, *Yours*, and not *mine*. It is the Spirit of Jesus and not the spirit of the world.

Holiness of life is not just obeying the rules. It is celebrating the joy of God's grace. Holiness, lived or preached, as a rules-oriented doctrine destroys joy. But holiness as celebration is not burdensome duty. It is not the lash of the taskmaster. The joy of serving a God who has given us more than we could ever pay back is holiness that dances in delight.

A mighty raja in ancient India had a gardener who was a chronic thief. The nobleman overlooked it for years because the gardener never stole anything very precious. Finally, however, he stole one of the family jewels. Prying a ruby of inestimable value out of the royal crown, the wicked gardener fled in the night.

In the dark, as he rode the nobleman's horse wildly out of the royal compound, he trampled the nobleman's son and killed him.

Some days later the raja's soldiers captured the wretched thief and killer.

The miscreant was hauled before the raja. The executioner's broad sword poised over his neck, the penitent thief cried, "Please, mighty master, have mercy on me. Don't kill me. If not for my sake, then for my wife and five children. I plead — don't kill me."

The great and gracious raja forgave him. He not only forgave him the thievery and the murder; he reinstated him as gardener.

Three months later the gardener was again hauled before the raja. He had stolen a nearly worthless cup from the royal kitchen.

The great raja said, "Bring the swordsman and cut his head off. Execute him here in my presence."

The gardener did not dare to plead for his life. Instead he said, "I deserve to die. I'm not complaining. But I don't understand. You forgive me for the death of your son and then execute me for the theft of a miserable kitchen utensil."

The raja said, "No. No, you really don't understand. I'm not executing you for the theft of a cup. I'm executing you for the sin of ingratitude." ■

Holiness must become a joyful, triumphant celebration of God's grace. Gratitude and contentment are the answers of holiness to the spirit of this age. The spirit of the world is the horseleach which cries, "More, more, more." The spirit of holiness looks up at the bleeding, dying form of Christ on the cross and acknowledges humbly, "It is more than I deserve. He *is* enough for me."

EPILOGUE

THE ANCIENT KING

A Parable

Noxious fumes bubbling up from some evil subterranean reservoir lay heavily upon the land. Wicked giants preyed mercilessly on travelers who passed their massive castles. The roads and forests were infested with brigands. Sorcerers and powerful enchantresses worked black magic to bring down noble kings and raise up wretched pretenders in their places.

In addition to these things, a plague came upon them. Mysterious deaths claimed thousands. Many of these who died had certainly lived in dark perversions, but some were innocent victims of a disease bred in infamy and spread in the life fluids of the walking dead.

Dreams and visions began to awaken in the people.

The staff of life was stricken as well. Money, stacked high in lead-lined vaults, began to shrink. Wizards were called to the palace, but none seemed to be able to stop it. Men counted their coins in horror, having less and less each time they counted.

Confusion reigned. Children sold their souls *and* their bodies for magic powder. Mothers murdered their babies. Babies grew up to murder their mothers. Nations rose and fell like the ticking of a clock, not by decades, but by days. An evil spell had been cast across the earth. From a dark and forbidding cave somewhere, some loathsome warlock had grasped the goodly place. He began to tighten the death-grip. Daily he increased the agony, always squeezing in a fist as cruel and cold as steel. The pitiful and fearsome screams and wails of the people went up in a chorus.

"Who can help us?" they screamed. "Who can help us break this nightmare power?"

Just as hope paled and it appeared certain that Evil was destined to win, itinerant minstrels appeared. Traveling from village to city to country square, they sang their strange canticles. These haunting melodies were called the "Songs of the Ancient King" or the Olde Music. The power of this Olde Music was mighty indeed.

Dreams and visions began to awaken in the people. Even small children began to sing the Olde Music, though they had never heard it before. These children also had dreams and visions.

"Under the rule of the Ancient King, we had none of these plagues," the people began to say among themselves. "Why did we cast Him off, anyway?"

No one could remember. They only knew that it had been so long now that many thought the Ancient King had never really ruled. Some even said there was no King. They said the Time of Wisdom was a myth. They claimed that plagues had always been the same and that they always would be.

But still the people sang the songs and dreamed the dreams until they were stirred as never before. Voices, strong and powerful voices, proclaimed that the Time of Wisdom had been real and not really so long ago. Like an old man rousing slowly from painful dreams to the smell of spring, an awakening began.

Then the people cried, "We would be as we were then. Some of us remember! We will go back to the Olde Music. We can make the Time of Wisdom come again."

"No," the minstrels said. "No. You must seek the Ancient King. He alone can send the Prince of Virtue and break the evil. He alone! Not you! Seek the King, and He will send the Prince."

"What can we do then?" complained the people. "Why did you sing these songs? Why pour the Olde Music into our ears and then tell us we cannot do it?"

"Because," the minstrels said, "if you try to make the Time of Wisdom come again, you will surely fail. The Olde Music, all the dreams, the visions of the Time of Wisdom, these were to awaken in you the effort to seek the Ancient King.

"Seek Him. He will send the Prince. Shake off your slumber. The Prince of Virtue will come."

Revival never comes because men decide to become more virtuous. Virtue comes when men rebel against virtueless times and seek the Lord their God. We cannot, with iron will and fierce determination, reshape our culture. We can break our will before God, and He will change our culture. In times past God has raised up voices to stir hearts for conviction, remorse, repentance and revival. When a people awaken to the true state of their virtuelessness and to the depravity of their culture, then they seek the Lord their God. ■

NOTES

Chapter 1

1. Karl Menninger, *Whatever Became of Sin?* (New York: Hawthorn Books Inc., 1973).
2. Ayn Rand, *The Virtue of Selfishness* (New York: Pearson Inc., New American Library, 1964).

Chapter 4

1. A.W. Tozer, *The Pursuit of God* (Harrisburg, Pa.: Christian Publications, 1948), p. 16.

Chapter 6

1. Richard Foster, *Money, Sex and Power* (San Francisco: Harper and Row, 1985), p. 26.
2. John Wesley, "The Use of Money," in *The Collected Works of John Wesley* (Chicago: Baker House, n.d.), p. 126.
3. Richard Foster, *Money, Sex and Power* (San Francisco: Harper and Row, 1985), p. 32.

Chapter 8

1. Alan Jay Lerner and Frederick Loewe, *Camelot* (New York: Random House, 1961), p. 80.

Chapter 10

1. William Edmund Barrett, *The Lilies of the Field* (New York: Doubleday, 1962).